Community Organizing

A Holistic Approach

Joan Kuyek

D1253693

Fernwood Publishing • Halifax & Winnipeg

Photographs: Tanya Ball
Editing and design: Brenda Conroy
Cover design: John van der Woude
Printed and bound in Canada by Hignell Book Printing

MIX
Paper from
responsible sources
FSC® C013916

Published in Canada by Fernwood Publishing
32 Oceanvista Lane
Black Point, Nova Scotia, B0J 1B0
and 748 Broadway Avenue, Winnipeg, Manitoba, R3G 0X3
www.fernwoodpublishing.ca

Fernwood Publishing Company Limited gratefully acknowledges the financial support of the
Government of Canada through the Canada Book Fund, the Canada Council for the Arts,
the Nova Scotia Department of Tourism and Culture, the Manitoba Department of Culture,
Heritage and Tourism under the Manitoba Publishers Marketing Assistance Program and the
Province of Manitoba, through the Book Publishing Tax Credit, for our publishing program.

Library and Archives Canada Cataloguing in Publication

Kuyek, Joan Newman, 1942-
Community organizing : a holistic approach / Joan Kuyek.

Includes bibliographical references.
ISBN 978-1-55266-444-5

1. Community organization--Canada.
2. Social action--Canada. 3. Community power--Canada.
4. Political participation--Canada. I. Title.

HM766.K89 2011   361.8'0971   C2011-902779-8

Contents

Part 4 Reclaiming the Economy,
Healing Our Relationship to the Earth

Part 5 Asserting Political Power

Part 6 Lessons Learned

Acknowledgements

A version of this book, *Fighting for Hope: Organizing to Realize our Dreams*, was published in 1990 by Black Rose Books. What started out as a revision has become more than that; the world has changed and I have more experience. I hope the perspectives and ideas in this book will be useful to activists and those who want to be.

This work has grown out of many conversations, readings, meetings, conferences and experiences. I don't believe that any ideas are truly "original": everything we think and do is built on the lives and words of our ancestors, human and otherwise. What can be unique is the cloth we weave from them. I am grateful for these opportunities to absorb what others have said and done; I only hope my words are worthy of those who have gone before me and those who will come after.

I am particularly grateful to Gayle Broad, Cathleen Kneen, Lynne Davis, Robert Clark and Devlin Kuyek, who read early drafts of the book for me and made many suggestions, most of which I have incorporated, and to Errol Sharpe of Fernwood Publishing for taking on the project.

My communities in Ottawa and Sudbury have sustained me throughout my adult life. My wonderful family always inspires me and gives me hope for the future.

This book is dedicated to my grandchildren:
Zev, Fanon, Una, Kelton and Brandon,
and to the memory of my Aunt Jean, who lived all her 100 years
with an open mind, integrity and courage.

Part 1

Understanding the Context

View of the Vale Inco smelter taken from Big Nickel Mine Road

1

Why This Book?

Working for community, for the healing and protection of the earth and for justice has organized my life in Canada for over forty years. Life as a community organizer has shaped my values and analysis of the world around me. This book is a product of that work and of the work of other organizers from all over the world.

At the base of community organizing is a belief that all people want to be able to deal with what life visits on them and their loved ones, and that all people want to create the changes they need and to resist those that hurt them. The power to make this happen is only possible when people work and act together.

Over centuries of human existence, peoples have organized themselves in different ways to accomplish the social project. For the last five thousand years — out of 150,000 years of modern human existence — cooperative and earth-based peoples have been conquered or dominated by peoples who were organized hierarchically and who treated the earth as a resource to be exploited. Most history is about the battles between rival hierarchies for power over resources, peoples and territories. The unwritten story of the last five thousand years is the efforts of ordinary people to resist this oppression and build some kind of life for themselves and their children despite the battles for power that have raged in their midst.

Resistance is not new. History is full of stories of the oppressed rebelling against the oppressor, only to create an equally oppressive system. What we learn from oppression is how to oppress. If we want a truly transformative politics, then we take up methods that embody the kind of world we want to create; we have to change deeply embedded beliefs and behaviours.

We are all a product of the culture we want to change; our strategies are based on a paradigm of competition and conquest. Doris Lessing points out that in times of war we are permitted to be brutal and cruel, and those of us who engage in the actual fighting often enjoy it. The "dreadful public elation" that comes with the culture of war is strong because war requires living in "that extreme of tension, alertness and danger"; it creates heroes; it speaks to our need to be significant; it allows us to act out our fear of the

Other.[1] If we want to construct a society that can live in harmony with the earth; that sees human beings as one part of creation, we have to understand and undo the destructive, hierarchical patterns we have internalized.

Starhawk writes:

> Domination is not the creation of some evil force, but the result of millions of human choices, made again and again over time. Just so can domination be undone, by shaping new choices, by small and repeated acts of liberation…. Domination is a system, and we are part of it, and in that lies hope. For any system is always in delicate balance, dependent for stability on the feedback of its parts. When the feedback changes, so does the system. At first it reacts to regain its stability, but if the new feedback is sustained, the system will be transformed.[2]

In Canada organizing is having a tough time. There is frustration with our inability, despite our activism, to halt the power and predations of the global economy. We feel overwhelmed by the number and complexity of issues that we are expected to deal with. People working for change in community groups, non-governmental organizations (NGOs), unions and campaigns are frequently unaware or dismissive of the efforts of other activists. We are fragmented and don't know what to do to be more effective. In the meantime, the political right has been gaining legitimacy, and our numbers appear to be shrinking.

It does not have to be this way. Indigenous cultures use a holistic paradigm called the "medicine wheel" to understand issues and to plan their activities. The Wheel can have many configurations, but one of the most common has culture and spirituality in the east, social relations in the south, physical relationships (environment and economy) in the west and administration and governance in the north. If we pay equal attention to all parts of the medicine wheel, our lives and communities will be in balance. This teaching applies to the work of activists in Canada. We may know how to organize in political parties, do cultural work, group process and political strategy, or create economic/environmental alternatives, but whole chunks of experience and information are often missing from our work. Like a wheel that has one or two flat sides, we are out of balance and our plans get stuck. To make the wheel turn again, we need to work holistically, to pay attention to all the quadrants of the wheel.

Organizing effectively is contextual; it is about using the collective power of people to shift and shape the cultural, economic, political and social aspects of the environment around us. How we analyze and understand the structures and characteristics of that environment determines our strategies. The better we know the context, the more effective we can be.

The current global context is a frightening one. The unfettered greed of globalization and the financial casino has deepened poverty and misery around the world, further weakened governments and strengthened a global elite. The welfare state is under attack. China (with its centralized government and economy) has emerged as a global power, owning most of the American debt and buying up resource properties around the world. The environmental crisis has intensified, as governments find themselves unable and unwilling to act to reverse climate chaos, pollution and the depletion of water and food supplies. Forced migration of entire populations has become endemic; civil wars, water shortages and famine threaten much of the world. In 2001, the destruction of the Twin Towers in New York launched the "war on terror," increasing state surveillance and public paranoia, justifying sophisticated spying and the suspension of hard-earned civil liberties, and creating new theatres of war.

Perhaps most disturbing has been the galloping epidemic of "hyper-individualism" amongst the affluent in the Western world. "We change religions, spouses, towns, professions with ease…. Our affluence isolates us even more. We are not just individualists; we are hyper-individualists such as the world has never known."[3] We believe we can create our own identities; we purchase services we used to exchange with our neighbours; we fail to understand the role of the public good and the commons; we reduce taxation and impoverish the state. We are lonely and we are afraid, and our fear makes us crave order and security. Political leaders that offer safety and simplistic analyses are gaining ground.

The past two decades have also seen the rise of the global justice movement, as the internet has become a valuable tool for research, networking and building solidarity. South African apartheid was defeated in 1990. The Berlin Wall came down. The Declaration on Indigenous Rights was passed at the UN. In Bolivia, an Indigenous mass-based movement came to power. Suharto's thirty-two-year reign of terror in Indonesia came to an end. Argentina threw out the World Bank and workers took over factories. Venezuela elected a socialist president, and Cuba survived the fall of the Soviet Union. The Zapatistas in Chiapas provided a new language for political transformation. In Canada, the events at Kahnasatake (Oka) and many subsequent assertions of sovereignty by Aboriginal peoples have energized the work, as Indigenous struggles around the world have inspired the vision of the global justice movement.

Peoples from around the globe have laid siege to transnational corporations and the institutions that serve them, gathering in unprecedented numbers outside the meetings of the powerful, from the World Trade Organization conference in Seattle to the meeting of the G20 in Toronto in 2010. All around the world, people have been working at the local, regional and national levels to create the changes they want to see in the world and to resist the predations of global capital. As Paul Hawken's research indicates, internationally there are now over a million organizations around the world working for ecological sustainability and social justice.[4]

Everywhere, there are activists who have learned and are learning how to put the creation of relationships and building of community at the heart of their efforts. They are building up the soil that will nourish real change. What they do "works." Change activities that work do the following:

- They create vision and enthusiasm so that many diverse people want to be committed to the work; they build a growing base of support for an equitable society.
- They make understanding about and effective work on key issues accessible to previously uninformed and inactive people.
- They create and model sustainable alternatives for the provision of food, shelter, energy, transportation and the care of children, the disabled and the elderly; they re-create and protect the "Commons."
- They establish multiplying numbers of relationships of respect for all beings and each other, kindness and dignity; they do not seek to increase public fear.
- By focusing on key contradictions in the system, they transform the power of predatory elites, redistribute wealth and establish equity.

Organizing is like making soup out of leftovers. We may be dreaming of bouillabaisse, but when we open the fridge and find some beans, a potato and an onion, we use our imagination and creativity to make the best soup we can. This book offers a number of methods and tools to build our capacity to make life sustaining soup. As the slogan from the World Social Forums said "Another World Is Possible." It is up to us to create it.

My Life as an Organizer

We never organize by ourselves; anything organizers accomplish is a product of time and place and the work of many different people. However, since the perspective of this book is a product of my history, let me tell you a little bit about my life as an organizer. I began my work in the "movement" in the midst of the tumult of the 1960s, as a researcher with the Company of Young Canadians (CYC), an attempt by the Canadian government to contain young radicals and put them into community service. Since I was a personable, young white woman, they hired me to interview national voluntary organizations to ask what they thought young Canadians should be doing. Some of the people I met in this work were to change my life.

First were a few experienced adult educators, who introduced me to something called "community development," and, because of the abysmal lack of knowledge about it in the CYC, I became in two short months the CYC's expert on it. Second were the student radicals in the Student Union for Peace Action. I fell in love with the movement. After five months, converted to participatory democracy and community action, I quit my job and went to work for $75 a month on the Kingston Community Project in Kingston, Ontario. The project members organized tenants' associations, a teenage drop-in centre, two residents' associations, a food co-op and a range of other activities with the people of Kingston. ATAK, the Kingston tenants' rights group, grew out of our efforts, and, when we realized that we had to change the law to get anywhere, I hitch-hiked around the province to convince groups in Ottawa, Toronto and other cities to form the Ontario Tenants' Association. In 1970, the Ontario Tenants' Association won rent control and tenant protection under the Ontario Landlord and Tenant Act.

Running for ATAK, I was even elected to city council as the "alderman" for St. Lawrence Ward. I have always felt that my real education came from those people in Kingston who had the patience to spend some time with me.[5]

During that time, the women's liberation movement started up; it felt like the logical extension of the work we already did. I became a lifelong feminist. Applying the learning from community organizing work and from the women's liberation movement to other activities just made sense. The principles were the same after all: helping people achieve their own goals, building cooperatives, taking care of the earth, taking care of one another.

In 1970 I moved to Sudbury — the country's biggest mining town at the height of a boom. Inco and Falconbridge, the two enormous mining companies that dominated the community, were expanding rapidly. Inco had 20,000 miners on its payroll, most of them young, from all over the country. We used to say that you could get stoned in the bar just by taking a deep breath, and the bars did a booming business. Within three years, the payroll had been reduced by half, and most of the young people followed the jobs to Alberta and Elliot Lake.[6]

Some of us started the first daycare centre in Sudbury in 1972. When I was a teller at the Royal Bank we tried to organize a union; we supported union organizing at lumber companies, department stores, white collar workers at Inco. Our Sudbury women's group put out a guide and a film for Sudbury women in crisis called *Alternatives to Hysteria*.[7] We demonstrated and submitted briefs about health care and abortion issues. My friend Sue Byron and I ran an unsuccessful but interesting bookstore called The Book Mine. During a nine-month strike at Inco in 1978–9, we organized strike support in the community and across the country.[8] Because people don't usually get paid to organize, I have worked in a variety of jobs over the years. Every one of them has been a great learning experience. I have worked in legal clinics, community colleges and universities, retail stores, the telephone company and nursing homes.[9] During that time, too, I raised two children of my own and a daughter by choice — experiences that taught me more than anything I ever learned from paid work.

In the 1980s, as the national staff person for a three-year project of the United Church of Canada called The Church and the Economic Crisis, I had the privilege of travelling across the country many times doing workshops to help people understand how the economy worked and assisting folk to develop programs for economic justice in their church and community.[10]

Later I became the half-time Canadian contact person for a program of the World Council of Churches, called the Urban-Rural Mission (URM). This creative program was a worldwide network of community organizers from all faiths (including animist, Judaism, Islam and atheists), committed to justice, peace and ecological integrity. My job was to create and maintain such a network in Canada. Because our funds were limited, we created a network of eighteen active organizers from across the country that met twice a year in different communities to share what they were learning from their work. Each person sat in the group for three years and then was replaced by another organizer on a rotational basis. A third of the members were Indigenous organizers, a third were from racialized groups and a third were Euro-Canadian (split evenly between Quebec and the rest of Canada). Annually, some of us travelled to other continents to meetings hosted by contact groups there. What a learning opportunity for all of us!

Following the URM, I was hired as the founding program coordinator for Sudbury Better Beginnings Better Futures, a community development program with the families in my own neighbourhood. Better Beginnings forced me to bring all that I had learned from other organizers and movement activists home: to weave these experiences into the equally valuable life lessons and wisdom of the people in my own city.

In 1998, exhausted by the Better Beginnings work, I was contracted for a year for the Urban Issues Program of the Samuel and Saidye Bronfman Family Foundation to travel across the country to help them evaluate one of the most innovative funding programs in Canada.

And then in 1999, I moved to Ottawa to lead the formation of MiningWatch Canada, a collaboration of many local, regional, national NGOs, battling the impacts of mining on communities in Canada and by Canadian mining companies around the world. I retired from the staff in spring 2008. Since then, I earn my living teaching in formal and informal settings.

Notes

1. Doris Lessing, "When in the Future They Look Back on Us." *Prisons We Choose to Live Inside,* CBC Massey Lectures, 1986.

2. Starhawk, *Truth or Dare* (New York: Harper and Row, 1987) p. 314. A holistic description and analysis of the state of the world, with ideas, exercises and incentives for working to change it.

3. Bill McKibben, *Deep Economy: The Wealth of Communities and the Durable Future* (New York: Holt Paperbacks, 2007) p. 96.

4. Paul Hawken, *Blessed Unrest: How the Largest Social Movement in History Is Restoring Grace, Justice and Beauty to the World* (New York: Penguin Books, 2007).

5. Richard Harris, *Democracy in Kingston: A Social Movement in Urban Politics 1965–70* (Montreal and Kingston: McGill-Queen's University Press, 1988). Provides a detailed history of the Kingston Community Project.

6. Jamie Swift, *The Big Nickel: Inco at Home and Abroad* (Toronto: Between the Lines, 1977). Provides a detailed history of Inco to 1976.

7. Women Helping Women, *Alternatives to Hysteria: A Guide to Sudbury Women in Crisis* (Sudbury, 1977).

8. Sophie Bissonnette, Joyce Rock and Martin Duckworth, *A Wives Tale,* 1980. A film about the organizing of Wives Supporting the Strike made during the 1978–9 strike.

9. Joan Kuyek, *The Phone Book: Working at Bell Canada* (Toronto: Between the Lines, 1979).

10. Joan Kuyek, *Managing the Household: A Handbook for Economic Justice Work* (Toronto: United Church of Canada, 1990). Records the learnings from the Economic Crisis project.

2

Understanding Power-Over

In 1987, I was in Taiwan, where I visited political prisoners jailed for twenty-five years for doing nothing more than advocating free elections, where I met workers who had been stabbed by company-employed thugs (at a Canadian-owned factory) for protesting layoffs and where I saw twelve- and thirteen-year-old Filipina and Indigenous girls who had to turn forty tricks a day just to keep from being murdered by their pimps.

Returning from that trip, I rode on the airplane beside a lean, fit man in blue jeans who told me he had just been in Seoul on business. He was an engineer at the Pentagon, and he had been there as part of a sales team, along with some generals. He said that he had replaced his passport three times that year, because he had visited so many different countries to sell military equipment. His next visit would be to Canada in April: he had a "deal" for the Canadian government on some radar equipment for the F-18 jet. He said he liked his work: it was interesting, challenging, and he really liked to visit all these foreign countries. He acted like he'd had a moral lobotomy.

There are real people who do real evil things in this world: they murder children, they torture and rape and steal from the poorest. They are willing to do anything to hold on to their money or their position. Then there are other people who make it possible for this evil to continue, sometimes profiting from it, sometimes with active support, sometimes unknowingly. Evil is made possible by their human labour, consent and ignorance.

For example, what is the relative responsibility of the following people if a nuclear bomb is dropped: the shareholders of the company that manufactured the bomb? The workers who assembled it? The miners who produced the uranium? The pilot who flew the plane? The wife of the pilot who let him go to work that day? The president of the country that issued the order to drop it? Those of us who protest in the streets against the bomb?

Don't tell me we are all equally responsible. We are not. Change is about the organization of the way power is distributed. "Politics" means the organization of power. There is a politics of the family, of the church, of the classroom and of the community just as there is a politics of the state or the global economy. When we talk about "getting power" or "power structures"

17

in community groups, we often find that people are uncomfortable with the discussion. "Power" is synonymous to them with domination and oppression, and they will deny that anyone in the group holds it or that they themselves seek it. Or they will protest that there are "no enemies," only people who need to be changed. The discussion gets confused and unhelpful.

When power becomes a dirty word, so that no one can name it or talk about it, then those who seek it can operate without controls on their behaviour. If we want to make the flow of power truly equal, then we have to understand it.[1]

In her important book, *Truth or Dare*, Starhawk names three distinct kinds of power: power-over, power-with and power-from-within. They are very different from one another.

- "Power-from-within" is the personal power each of us has, our energy, self-knowledge, self-discipline, character.
- "Power-with" sees the world as made up of changing relationships and is our collective energy and ability to act together. It includes influence and leadership as legitimate forms of power.
- "Power-over," on the other hand, requires the domination or oppression of others. Unlike the other two forms, "it has to have a clear material base, as it is grounded in the ability to punish by imposing physical or economic sanctions."[2]

The goal of community organizing has to be the transformation of the institutions and practices of "power-over" to relationships of "power-with." By allowing ourselves to be dominated we collude with power-over. Every act of freedom — at home, at work, in our relationships — diminishes the strength of the power structure.

Power-over is not confined to large structures, it can exist anywhere that some people have access to the material means of dominating someone else: in the family, the school, the church, in a social change organization. As long as some people have the ability to control the lives of others, they have the ability to use power-over.

What are the characteristics of power-over? Power-over is a process based in control of capital, resources, military force and government, and it is structured in a hierarchy of domination. It is not monolithic. Its very nature means that those at the top of the hierarchy compete with one another and those further down the ladder compete for the favours of those above them. It cannot function without the hired labour of the people who work to maintain it and without the submission of the majority of the dominated. Power-over creates fear not only in the oppressed but in the oppressor. It is that fear that stimulates those with power-over to react with force against any indications of resistance or rebellion. Power-over corrupts all who use it to control others.

The World Economic System

The most pervasive form of power-over is found in the world economic system, precisely because power-over depends on control of capital, resources and force. In capitalist countries like Canada, the very purpose of the economy is to provide the accumulation of capital and power for the owners of private corporations, the shareholders. The greatest limitation of this economic system is that it can only measure and record services and things that have monetary value (in dollars, yen, rubles). If the benefits are not measurable in money, then they are deemed not to exist. The success of any enterprise or activity is judged by its ability to show an excess of measurable benefits over costs. "Economy" comes from two Greek words, meaning "to manage the household." We can all imagine what would happen if a person only paid attention to the money coming in and out of the home. There would be no way to value love, beauty, cooking, composting, sharing with neighbours and family. Those things that really mattered, but could not be measured in dollars, would not count.

WE only see $

The world economy is shaped by the decisions of human beings in corporations and states and is made possible by the day-to-day work we all do. It is dependent upon consenting human labour, an assumption of unending resources and smoothly functioning technologies. It functions because people are "just doing their job."

cogs

The basic organizational unit of our society is the corporation. In law, corporations are treated as legal persons, although they might be made up of thousands of workers.[3] Corporations are designed in a hierarchical fashion to facilitate control from the pinnacle and rapid response from the bottom of the pyramid. Each corporation, like each household, maintains its own ledger, and a healthy corporation is considered to be one where income exceeds expenditure. In a corporation, the only way to measure job satisfaction is in terms of higher productivity, and the only way to measure impact on the environment is through potential loss of income to the corporation. Although concern is often expressed for other factors, there is no way to have them enter into the company accounting system; they are "externalities." Because companies make profits by keeping costs down, keeping wages low is one of their concerns. If there is lots of competition for scarce jobs and/or the rate of unionization is low, they benefit. The film *The Corporation* explores the problems with this organizational form and comes to the conclusion that corporations, as "persons," are psychopaths.

corp = ppl

externalities

As an example, Vale Inco — a Brazilian multinational mining company — now owns the numerous nickel mines, smelters and copper and nickel

[handwritten margin note: expected corp -only care for $]

refineries in Sudbury. Since its founding as the Mond Nickel Company over a hundred years ago, the Sudbury complex has been a profitable enterprise. The success of the company however has been built on the theft of the lands of the Atikameksheng Anishnabek,[4] the destruction of over 80,000 hectares[5] of white-pine forest, the production of war materials that were sold to both sides during the First and Second World Wars,[6] ignoring at best state terror in Guatemala and Indonesia during the time the company was expanding in these countries,[7] and working conditions that have resulted in cancer, crippling back injuries, white-hand or deafness for the majority of its workforce. For years, its "super-stack" was the single largest source of acid rain in North America[8]; and the soils in the area have been seriously compromised by lead, copper, nickel, cadmium, selenium and arsenic.[9] As a response to public pressure, the company has developed a method for reclaiming the sulphur dioxide that it produces from the air: it sells it for fertilizer, which is almost as destructive to the environment. It only became attractive economically to the company to reduce emissions when it found it could market the reclamation technology and the sulphur to other companies.

Most of the real environmental and justice costs of the enterprise do not appear on the Vale Inco ledger: they are either completely unrecorded or they end up on the ledgers of individual households or in the "social programs" of governments. Vale is one of three mining companies in Ontario that does not have to post a cash bond with the Ontario government against the cost of eventual reclamation. It has only a line on its balance sheet to protect the community against the cost of the clean-up that will follow its inevitable closure.[10] The Canadian economic system is "advanced capitalism." With a few exceptions, control is in the hands of transnational corporations, like Vale Inco, owned outside the country. The base of Canadian wealth is the mining of the earth's resources: fossil fuels, fish, lumber, metals, soil. Most secondary industries are related to these primary products.[11]

Worldwide, Canada is the sixth highest consumer of energy[12] and the second highest producer per capita of waste,[13] most of it due to the enormous energy requirements and waste byproducts of resource extraction industries from corporate agriculture to oil sands mining. As with Vale Inco, the business response is to deal with the problem by creating new technologies and businesses that will enable consumption to continue at this unsustainable rate. One example is pumping carbon dioxide underground into depleted oil wells.

A very few people in Canada, the owners of the large multinational companies, become rich by extracting wealth from the rest of us. Canada had only twenty-five billionaires in March 2008.[14] In 2007, Lars Osberg reported: "All the gains in growth since 1980 have been received by the top 10% of the (population) distribution... the further up one goes, the larger

[handwritten: Rich get rich / poor get poor]

the rate of gain." He found that although the median net worth of the top 10 percent of the population went from $557,500 to $1.24 million in 2005, the bottom 10 percent saw their net worth slip from minus $2,200 to minus $10,000.[15]

In Canada, the Canadian Council of Chief Executives is the organization that represents the interests of the corporate leaders.[16] It works vigorously to persuade governments to implement the corporate agenda, which includes deeper economic and security integration with the United States, privatization of health care, cutbacks in the social security network, reduction of the minimum wage, voluntary environmental standards, the hobbling of trade unions and the restriction of dissent. *[handwritten: uncle mile Socialism]*

Canada's extractives sector plays a predator role in the Global South with the full support of our government. Mining and oil companies receive tax incentives and subsidies to extract resources from Latin America, Africa and Asia. In international forums, Canada opposed the Declaration on the Rights of Indigenous People, as well as bans on asbestos and nickel batteries and limits on carbon emissions, and consistently advocates trade agreements that will further impoverish the one billion people in the world who are facing starvation.

With our own needs, desires and visions, each of our lives becomes a battleground between different balance sheets. The corporations want our time, our dollars and our energy. When we have trouble getting to meetings or being loving to our friends and families, when we have to spend three hours a day getting to and from work or are always having to move to find affordable housing or work, these are economic and political problems, not "social" ones. The problems of our economic system are located in the very real stuff of our lives.[17]

[handwritten: Econ = Lives ≠ $]

Power Over in Other Forms

[handwritten: Institutional Bullying]

In addition to the economic system, power-over is exercised in other ways. For many of us, fear of physical injury, pain and humiliation are a way of life. Bullying — the use of force for dominance — has many forms: wars and genocide, spousal abuse, homophobia, racism, gangs, schoolyard power struggles. It is also a key feature of our institutions.

We live in a world that is ripped apart by wars. For many Canadians, immigrants and those who have relatives and friends living in war-torn countries, war is not remote. The twentieth century was the bloodiest since the conquest of the Americas by European powers. It is estimated that 240 million people died in wars in the twentieth century.[18] Canada has become a global military power, engaging actively in the war in Afghanistan. By 2007–8, Canada's military spending was more than $18 billion per year, and we had become the thirteenth highest military spender in the world.[19]

[handwritten: Canada is at war]

By far the most prevalent violence in Canada is against women, and most is from our partners. Statistics Canada reports that seventy-five women were killed by their partner in 2004 and that 7 percent of women experienced spousal abuse between 1999 and 2004. In the same period 24 percent of Aboriginal women reported being physically abused by their partner.[20] Aboriginal women also suffer disproportionately from the violence of strangers.

Women who want to become active in the community or the workplace can face the damaged pride of their husbands and boyfriends. Often they are risking their lives. Or they are risking being beaten or shunned by their families for breaking with the traditional role of women. Sometimes they are said to be unfit mothers and their children are taken from them.[21] When women lay charges or fear for their lives or their children, they have to leave home; they become dependent on welfare and the police for protection. In most cases they have to live in transition houses or go into hiding, while the batterer walks the streets.

There can be little doubt that the state treats Blacks, Arabs and Indigenous people differently than Caucasians. Aboriginal justice inquiries in Alberta, Manitoba and Nova Scotia produced scathing indictments of the justice system in those provinces in the late 1980s, and there have been subsequent inquiries into racialized police brutality in Montreal, Nova Scotia, Saskatchewan and British Columbia. Since 9/11, Islamophobia is targeting large numbers of our population.

The Canadian state has never hesitated to move swiftly and viciously whenever social control breaks down. The state's reaction against the Winnipeg General Strike, the Estevan Strike, the On to Ottawa Trek, the resistance of Doukhobours, the October Crisis in Quebec in 1970 and the Squamish Five are only a few of the more shocking incidents in Canada's history.[22]

Since Europeans came to North America, Aboriginal peoples have been engaged in a struggle to protect their traditional lands, a struggle they have waged almost entirely with non-violent direct action. The response of the Canadian state and the provincial governments (with some exceptions) has been to intimidate with military strength, as the following numerous examples attest: Oka, Temagami, Burnt Church, Akwesasne, Burnt Church, Ipperwash, Gustefson Lake and Kitchenuhmaykoosib Inninuwug.

Violence Against the Poor

At a workshop on the feminine face of poverty in Sudbury, we were looking at the situation of a single parent on family benefits and trying to diagram all the forces that serve to disorganize her life. We talked about transportation scheduling and the location of housing, credit and costly medications and her children's inability to participate in school activities and recreation. And

Institutional racism exists (handwritten margin note)

then her voice broke. "The worst part," she said, "is when it's the last week of the month and you find out they are holding your cheque."

Canada has an elaborate system of welfare for those who are unable to earn a living through wage labour. It has been there since relief and the dole in the thirties. Working people and organizations of the unemployed fought hard to get it: riding the rails and getting shot up on the On to Ottawa Trek, demonstrating and lobbying and struggling in elections. It is kept in place by the continuous vigilance of the ordinary folk in this country. When an effort was made to change the old age pension, seniors across the country mobilized and demonstrated on Parliament Hill. In the 1990s — with the onslaught of neoliberalism, capitalism's latest manifestation, in Canada — every province tried to gut their welfare system, and thousands of people dropped what they were doing to petition, lobby, demonstrate and organize. That the cutbacks were not worse is a tribute to their efforts. *— Ppl can make a Difference*

A lot of people make their living as helpers in the welfare system: social workers, income maintenance officers, psychologists, family therapists, administrators, book-keepers, clerks and so on. But there are also a lot of other interests that benefit: computer manufacturers and paper and communications companies sell to the administrative apparatus. And then there are all the merchants, gas companies, landlords and services where welfare cheques are spent. Even on skid row, there are pawn shops, barber colleges, Christian missions, used clothing and furniture stores, cheque cashing outfits and rooming house/hotels. And poor people also pay taxes; in fact they pay a higher percentage of their income in taxes than the rich do. Welfare is an important part of our economy.[23] *Welfer => trikldown Econ*

The government has transformed demands for redistribution of wealth *fails to move Power* into a punitive and complex system that serves other interests better than it serves the poor. Although it provides a minimal income to most poor people in Canada, it does little to shift wealth from those who have to those who don't, and nothing at all to redistribute power.

Most social policy in Canada "blames the victim" and maintains the powerlessness of the bottom 20–30 percent of the population. Even our much-vaunted job creation programs are short-term, minimum wage, undercapitalized efforts that serve to shift the costs of unemployment from one government ledger to another. Most training programs for the unemployed fill the needs of industry. Although they might move some individuals from unemployed to employed categories, they do nothing to change the percentage of the population without paid work.

The welfare system takes what might once have been the concept of "caring for your neighbour as yourself" and creates a set of relationships where some people get to be professional helpers and others get to be professional helpees. Which we get to be is determined by our race, income and birth as much as it is by our abilities.[24] That's because we have to go to secondary school or college or university to get to be a helper, and that costs money. On the other hand, low-income people get to be the helpees, and they are trained in the school of hard knocks.

We would think that people never did know how to get along with one another or to solve human problems before the advent of the social worker. People no longer get together to stop someone from beating his kids; they call in the Children's Aid Society. People who are in despair or emotional pain are treated by psychologists and psychiatrists and drugs. Some welfare families see five or more social workers or services at one time. Every one of these services has different rules, structures and powers that make them confusing and frightening, even to the most sophisticated helpee.

Often the central message communicated by these services is that the client does not have sufficient skills to get along, that they have to depend on the good will of professionals to survive and that they had better be "good" (however that is defined by the agency) or they will be punished: be institutionalized, have their kids taken away, be kicked out of the program and so on. The client's own survival skills and street smarts are devalued and undermined. On the other hand, the system is also hard on the professional helpers. Day after day, they see people in crisis that they have only limited ability and power to help. The burn-out rate amongst workers in the helping professions is very high.[25]

The welfare system itself doesn't even pretend to "help" the poor anymore. Now it calls its frontline workers "income maintenance officers," and they administer files, interview clients and act like fraud police. For many welfare recipients, the fear of getting cut off and potentially ending up starving and homeless, or losing their children because they cannot support them any longer is a very real threat.

The amount of social assistance received in real dollars has been shrinking for a number of years, and the only way that most recipients survive is to earn income babysitting or at part-time work or to have a boyfriend on the side or a secret roommate. Undeclared income is a criminal offence for someone on welfare, as are other means of income supplement — theft, pushing drugs, bootlegging and prostitution.

> In April 2001, Sudbury resident Kimberly Rogers was convicted of welfare fraud for receiving student loans while collecting social assistance. The money helped pay for four years of community college. She earned a diploma in social services in April 2000. The welfare office determined an overpayment of $13,468.31.
>
> After her conviction, she was automatically suspended from receiving social assistance benefits for three months. She was sen-

tenced to: six months of house arrest with no money to pay the rent; allowed out of her apartment only three hours a week, except with permission "for shopping for necessities of life" although she had no money to do so; expected to repay $13,468.31; 18 months probation; loss of the right to have part of her student loan forgiven; and, of course, no income at all for three months.

At the time of her conviction, Kimberly Rogers was five months pregnant and was suffering from a number of medical conditions for which she required prescribed medication. When her benefits were cancelled, her Ontario Works prescription drug card was also cancelled.

She launched a Charter Challenge and got an injunction temporarily re-instating her benefits in May, but even after her benefits were reinstated Kimberly Rogers did not have enough money to support herself and her unborn child. She received Ontario Works Benefits of $520 per month, minus $52 to repay the overpayment. Her rent was $450 per month, leaving $18 a month for food and everything else. Ms Rogers could not access, nor could she afford, fresh fruits, vegetables, or meat on a regular basis.

She was alone and pregnant, with no money. Is deprivation of basic needs a suitable penalty for any crime? On August 9, 2001 Kimberly Rogers and her unborn child were found dead in her apartment.[26] → ppl have a right to life –

To impoverished people, the social safety net looks like an irrational system of spying and terror. For them to stick their necks out and organize with one another under these conditions takes great courage indeed.

John Kenneth Galbraith coined the term, the "culture of contentment" in 1992 to describe affluent North America.[27] He argued that middle-class America (including those of us living in Canada) had developed a culture that identified comfort as its most important value. To achieve this, the middle classes surround themselves with creature comforts and refuse to look at anything that might threaten their sense of well-being. Amongst these threats is the growing numbers and misery of the world's poor, on whose backs the affluence is built. The impoverished become a marginalized and excluded class, what Galbraith called the "underclass." The fear of being cast into the underclass — which is portrayed as miserable, violent and hopeless — keeps the middle classes from stepping outside their comfort zone into the lives of others. Sang Chul Lee, a former moderator of the United Church, a Korean who had been an exile three different times in this life, said "Canadians are paralyzed by their fear of being poor."

middle class
kept in line for fear of becoming "poor'

25

Notes

1. Starhawk, *Truth or Dare* (New York: Harper and Row, 1987) p. 314.
2. Starhawk, *Truth or Dare*, p. 16.
3. This is explored effectively in Mark Achbar, Jennifer Abbott and Joel Bakan, *The Corporation* (film), 2003. Available for purchase from their website <Thecorporation.com>.
4. Chief Arthur Petahtegoose, *Path of Destruction*, a radio documentary produced by Asad Ismi, 2008.
5. The SARA Group, *Sudbury Area Risk Assessment* vol. III, ch. 6.0, p. 6–14, 2009.
6. Jamie Swift, *The Big Nickel: INCO at Home and Abroad* (Toronto: Between the Lines, 1977).
7. Jamie Swift, *The Big Nickel*.
8. Jurgen Schmandt, Judith Clarkson and Hilliard Roderick (eds.), *Acid Rain and Friendly Neighbours* (Durham, NC: Duke University Press, 1988) p. 133.
9. The SARA Group, *Ecological Risk Assessment*, 2009 <http://www.sudburysoilsstudy.com/EN/indexE.htm>.
10. MiningWatch Canada, information from Ontario Ministry of Northern Development and Mines following a request under the Information and Privacy Act, List of Closure Plans using Corporate Financial Test as the Form of Financial Assurance (April 2006).
11. Roger Hayter and Trevor J. Barnes, "Canada's Resource Economy," *Canadian Geographer* 45, 1, 2001, p. 36–41.
12. (9.9 exajoules annually). Environment Canada, downloaded from <http://tiff.net/templates/learning/docs/THE_PLANET_StudyGuide.pdf> p. 17.
13. 2.2 kg per person per day. *Toronto Environmental Handbook '99*, quoted at <http://www.zubicks.com>.
14. CBC, "Canada's Super Rich," March 6, 2008, from <http://www.cbc.ca/news/background/wealth/>.
15. Lars Osberg, "A Quarter Century of Income Inequality in Canada 1981–2006," *CCPA*, 2007, p. 23–25 (using constant 2007 dollars).
16. The structure of the "Canadian Corporate Elite" has been carefully studied by researchers like Naomi Klein, William Carroll, John Porter, Jorge Niosi, and Wallace Clement.
17. Jesuit Centre for Social Faith and Justice, "Understanding Economics, Starting with Our Lives," *The Moment*, Spring, 1989.
18. Velcrow Ripper, *Fierce Light* (film), Seville Pictures in co-production with the National Film Board of Canada, 2008 <www.fiercelight.org>.
19. Stephen Staples and Bill Robinson, "More Than the Cold War: Canada's Military Spending 2007–2008," *CCPA Foreign Policy Series*, 2, 3 (October) 2007.
20. Statistics Canada, "Violence Against Women in Canada… by the Numbers" 2009 <http://www42.statcan.ca/smr08/smr08_012-eng.htm>.
21. C. Rodriguez and L. Wise, "Organizing with Women of Colour," a paper presented to URM North America, October 1989.
22. Pat Bird, *Of Dust and Time and Dreams and Agonies* (Willowdale, ON: John Deyell Company, 1975).
23. James Ward, *Organizing for the Homeless* (Ottawa: Canadian Council on Social

Development, 1989). Full of examples from first-hand experience, this book is a good mix of practical organizing ideas and theoretical analysis.

24. Malcolm Gladwell, *Outliers* (New York: Little, Brown and Company, 2008).

25. Ben Carniol, *Case Critical: Social Services and Social Justice in Canada*, fifth edition (Toronto: Between the Lines, 2007).

26. The Elizabeth Fry Society, "Dedicated to Kimberley Rogers," 2009. <http://www.elizabethfry.ca/rogers/2.htm>.

27. John Kenneth Galbraith, *The Culture of Contentment* (Boston: Houghton-Mifflin, 1993).

Part 2

Creating a Culture of Hope

Children admiring their Show of Hands fence sculpture

3

A Neighbourhood Rebuilds Itself

In 1991, the N'swakamok Native Friendship Centre in Sudbury hired me to be the founding program coordinator for an innovative community project in my own neighbourhood — the Sudbury Better Beginnings Better Futures project. The project is in the Donovan-Flour Mill areas. Sudbury, like many mining towns, has high unemployment rates, a lot of single parent families and one of the highest rates of death from cancers and accidents in the country. The project neighbourhood is culturally split — 38 percent francophone, 11 percent Aboriginal and the remaining Anglophone population is made up of people of many different European origins. At the time the project started, Sudbury was not a centre for immigrant settlement, as the mines were not hiring. The area was, and continues to be, one of the most disadvantaged in Ontario, despite the enormous profits and high incomes generated by the mines and smelters. When we started up, there were no services for families. Two playgrounds had been shut down three years before — the city's response to repeated vandalism. There was a closed school, where over $13,000 was spent annually to replace vandalized windows. Most of the landscape was barren, with dead grass and litter where children might have played.

A "conjunctural moment" in Ontario made the Sudbury project possible.[1] During the 1980s, there had been growing demand from communities and from professionals who worked with troubled children for "prevention" programs that would intervene with families in the early years through community-based activities. In response, a coordinated group of creative female Ontario public servants conceived of and developed a neighbourhood-based pilot program that combined parent involvement and early childhood activities. The pilot was to be a longitudinal research study that would follow the children for twenty-five years to see how the program affected them. The program was called Better Beginnings Better Futures.

In the late 1980s, a competition was held to determine which communities would get the $250,000 a year funding for five-year pilot projects. To compete, communities had to be low-income, had to bring together extensive partnerships of social agencies and had to have a plan for "community involvement." In the end, eleven communities were chosen, and Sudbury's Donovan-Flour Mill neighbourhood was one.

The Sudbury project had been initiated and led by the N'Swakamok Native Friendship Centre, but it was for all the cultures in the neighbourhood. The Aboriginal organization proved to be crucial to the later success of the project. N'Swakamok was a leader in Aboriginal programming, a pioneer in alternative schooling, court worker programs and the provision of effective family services. Most importantly, the leadership at N'Swakamok deeply believe in inclusion… that we live in an ever-expanding circle in which all cultures can learn to live in harmony. They also believe that people can change; that given half a chance, we can all do better. Anishinaabe culture came to infuse everything that Better Beginnings did and still does today. *[handwritten margin note: inclusion / multiculturism]*

The Sudbury Project was possible, and evolved differently than the other Better Beginning projects, because of the long activist history of so many people in the community. The neighbourhood was home to (Indigenous and non-Indigenous) people who had worked tirelessly on welfare reform, housing, youth concerns and solidarity with First Nations issues and strike support. The project benefitted from the links we had to provincial, national and global organizations and movements. It began only a few short months after the Oka crisis had rocked our world. In Sudbury, the Citizens Network in Support of Native Rights had worked with the traditional Aboriginal leadership to show the powers in Ottawa that we supported the resistance of the Aboriginal people. During the crisis, we had taken part in almost daily vigils, demonstrations and sunrise ceremonies. Our neighbourhood had sophisticated and creative leadership; we had ideas and, now, we had money.

The N'Swakamok Friendship Centre had a long history of working with local agencies to get the services they needed for their people, and they did this from a position of authority. In developing the proposal for Better Beginnings, the centre was able to entice agencies into trying a collaborative model. They used a "medicine wheel approach," which integrated and addressed the social, cultural, economic, environmental and political aspects of the lives of community members. They understood that all aspects of life were related.

N'swakamok also made sure that leaders from the low-income community were identified and involved in planning the project from the beginning. This was not easy: there were serious tensions with some of the agency representatives, who thought they knew more than community members, and with community leaders, who were used to getting their way with bullying tactics. And there were tensions between and within different parts of the community: between francophones and Aboriginal language needs, between people who lived in one part of the neighbourhood and another, between different families and so on. *[handwritten margin note: tensions run high]*

The provincial funding requirements meant that at least 50 percent of the governance of the project had to be from parents of children in the programs; it committed us to the longitudinal research; and it also committed us to providing services for children in the target age group. In the Sudbury case, this was four to eight year olds. In return, we would get $250,000 a year for five years for programming, with a minimal number of strings attached.

Once we knew we had the funding, we plunged in. The circle of agency representatives and community leaders that had put the proposal together continued to meet and develop the "vision statement":

> To promote and strengthen personal growth focused on the child and the individual uniqueness of all members within the community of Better Beginnings Better Futures. To promote and encourage active participation in all aspects in the shaping of programs and support systems, while integrating respect, and teamwork of everyone in achieving a safe, healthy and wholesome environment for all.

The leadership from the Aboriginal community ensured that we worked with all sections of the medicine wheel (cultural, environmental, political and economic) to develop leadership and capacity in the local community, and to face very tough questions about how we held everything in balance. Deciding our future meant questioning how we did things in the present and asking serious questions whenever we had to make decisions about programming:

- Social and cultural: What do we mean by inclusivity and tolerance? What is the role of cultural identity?
- Environmental: How do we learn to live carefully on the earth? And to change our environmental behaviour?
- Economic: How do we transform an economy that trashes the earth, impoverishes and creates inequality?
- Political: How do we create power to resist change that harms and creates the good changes we want to see for our children?

Our programs grew into being through a complex back-and-forth with different parts of the community and through — often wild — experimentation.

At first the circle was composed of one half agency reps and one half community members. But within a few years, the agency reps were reduced to those who lived in the neighbourhood. We decided to have a council with caucuses for francophone, Aboriginal and anglophone interests, and a fourth caucus — multicultural — to provide a forum for the tiny number of other racialized people in the neighbourhood. Each caucus would elect two persons to the council, and two others would be elected at large. Staff also sent two representatives to the council. The co-chairs were elected by all the members, and the council would work by consensus. The association would build relationships between people in the neighbourhood, strengthening mutual aid and interdependence. It would identify and build the capacity of leaders. And it would provide the programs people wanted for their kids.

We hired four community development workers, who had never worked in this capacity, from the local neighbourhood and set out to contact as many community people as we could — mostly using a "snowball approach": "Who else in the neighbourhood do you think I should talk to?"

Our first office was a cubby hole on the third floor of the Friendship Centre. We had a struggle to find any public space in the neighbourhood to meet. At last, we began holding weekly meetings at O'Connor Park — a dank and mouldy hockey shack — where the playground itself was closed. We provided food at each meeting, held them at times that worked for local people, and slowly, the numbers who turned up began to grow. Using a community mapping methodology, we worked with local people to identify what they wanted to see for their children.

Agency reps came to many of the meetings. Although most were respectful and did not intimidate local leaders, some problems were evident. For example, a woman who had dealt with an agency worker as a client found it difficult to express her opinions about anything when that worker was there but would be very chatty when the worker was absent. Historically, agencies viewed the neighbourhood folk as clients and patients. They tended to think that what the people wanted was therapeutic services like money management and anger management.

But many of the people in the community were survivors who had gone through horrific life stresses. They were potential leaders, taking care of their families and one another with neither support nor recognition. When they were asked what they wanted for their children, they wanted concrete services like better public transit, better and more affordable housing, good schools, daycare, etc. They knew exactly what they wanted. So we set out to make this possible in any way we could.

Our first act was to set up an after-school program at O'Connor Park. This concrete-block hockey shack sat on a large patch of dead grass in the heart of the neighbourhood. When we asked the Recreation Department for the regular use of the facility, we were turned down, because it was to be used as a locale for city-wide hockey. Hockey would mean that local kids and families could not use the building. They could not afford the equipment or the fees, and most did not even have skates or know how to skate. On top of that, the canteen would tempt their kids with junk that they could not afford.

So we decided to just take over the building for the programs that the neighbourhood needed. One day, after a meeting, we just kept the key and started running an after-school drop-in, serving a nutritious snack, hiring a couple of local people who were excellent with children to supervise and create activities for the kids, and providing a family event on Hallowe'en. At first, the city didn't notice. Then, one day, city officials turned up with the huge fibreglass hockey boards.

We called everyone we knew to come to the park and told the city workers that we would not let the hockey boards go up. They went away. That evening and the next day, we painted the walls white and floors yellow, put curtains up in the change rooms and turned the hockey shack into a rather odd community centre. We met with the city and pushed for the after-school program. We got our agency partners to intervene. And we won. Although the boards went up eventually, the city hockey teams never came. We set up a skate library with used skates and found people to help local kids and their parents learn to skate. We served good community meals and ran imaginative activities for the kids. They loved it, and so did their parents.

At a workshop held that fall for all the different Better Beginnings sites, we had watched Nancy Brown of Seneca College do a presentation on playground planning. Nancy showed pictures of the standard equipment in playgrounds — red, yellow and blue plastic, with a slide, a climber and a tiny roofed area, built on sand with a chain link fence — with no children whatsoever playing on it. And then she showed pictures of Dufferin Grove Park and Spiral Garden in Toronto — with completely different ideas of play. In these environments, children could play behind small knolls — where they thought they were beyond the vision of supervising adults. There were lots of loose materials and equipment. There were water play structures with moveable bamboo piping, and plants and trees and shade, and there were adults interacting with them, sharing art, music, drama and stories. We invited Nancy to come to Sudbury and help us redesign O'Connor Park.

Nancy brought Paul Hogan of The Chong, a participatory guerilla art project in Toronto in the 1990s, with her. Paul was an artist, with a wild imagination and a love of play. Paul and Nancy had designed a program for the kids in the ravine at the back of the Hugh MacMillan Centre in Toronto called The Spiral Garden.[2] The Spiral Garden used the wooded beauty of the ravine to immerse children in nature. Artists from the outside community were brought in to work with the children in a program that used stories and myths to stretch their imagination and hands-on activities to allow them to create and work together. The program included gardening and fence weaving and homemade ritual. It even had a professional storyteller who would spin the children's experiences in the Garden into myth.

Having Paul and Nancy come to Sudbury in the spring of our first year (1992) was a cultural shock to some of the neighbourhood leadership. No one had met anyone like Paul before. He had us walk O'Connor Park looking for its "centre of power." This was identified in the middle of the large fenced area of dead wet grass, where the irrigation pipes had been leaking for years. He had us look at the rocky hill that rose on the south side of the park and proclaimed this as the mountain which governed the area. He challenged us to imagine the "myth" of the neighbourhood and to envision what the park might be. Nancy gave us all sorts of ideas for programming that would bring the children into touch with the natural world and that would awaken their sense of wonder and imaginations. We were blown away.

Very excited, we set out to transform O'Connor. The children were engaged in imagining a different kind of park. We built a sort of architectural model with movable pieces (trees, berms, a bandshell, a pool, a fire pit, vegetable and flower gardens, a rink, gardens, etc.) so that the kids could play with them and develop their ideas. They did drawings and told of their dreams for the park. And then we had a community meeting to decide on the final plan. We took it to the city and lobbied for changes. We won. Within a few years, the park was redesigned with sloping berms, a fire pit, real grass, walkways, a water park and — eventually — a completely remodelled community centre. In the winter, the whole neighbourhood turns out to skate.

But the power structures we need to change also exist in the local community: these are rough and tumble places, full of bullies. We had struggles around getting access to another underused community centre in the area, over power on the Better Beginnings council, over shifting existing power dynamics in the local community. Bullies would try to boss the programs at the different sites. There were inter-family battles and the use of Children's Aid as a weapon in neighbour-to-neighbour fights. The anglophones acted with entitlement and said really offensive things about other cultures. The francophone program said the smell of the sage burned when the Ojibwe staff started a meeting was offensive. Some of the francophone parents were afraid to meet with the French school principal because "their French wasn't good enough." The Aboriginal council members were upset when the francophones insisted on speaking French in a meeting (even with translation) and felt it diminished the importance of Ojibwe. It was never easy.

We worked to establish as many culturally appropriate programs as we could: French language early-bird and after-school programs, French school-based programs, a family Aboriginal camp on the land owned by the Friendship Centre, beading workshops during the after-school programs, participation with the Friendship Centre in sweat lodges and workshops, Ojibwe in the schools.

Some of us had a dream that we could somehow assist in re-birthing the authentic parts of the cultures in the neighbourhood — undoing advertising culture. This was an ongoing struggle. At St. Gabriel School, the kids redecorated the standard tables and metal chairs they had in the lunchroom with spatter painting and their own wild designs and then some of the staff proudly painted TV cartoon characters on the walls.

Perhaps most important was the development of Myths and Mirrors Community Arts in 1995. The brainchild of Laurie McGauley, a community member, Myths and Mirrors uses collectively developed arts to build community, challenge cultural assumptions and inspire hope. At the heart of their work is the genuine respect they always show for the people they organize with, whether they are punks, skaters or seniors. They worked with the neighbourhood through "performance art, murals, mosaics, music and drumming, gardens, celebrations, rituals, stilting, face painting, costuming, visual arts, installations, video, film, games and popular education."[3] Myths and Mirrors drew their inspiration from groups like Bread and Puppet Theatre in Toronto and from the popular theatre work of Augusto Boal.

Myths and Mirrors played an important role in helping us work out neighbourhood tensions and differences, creating a culture particular to the neighbourhood that was playful, consensus-based and respectful of needs and responsibilities. Myths and Mirrors organized all sorts of collective projects in the neighbourhood: giant puppet shows, celebrations of seasons, decorating all the buildings with collective murals and art, undertaking murals with the roughest teens in the neighbourhood, creating community gardens. Myths and Mirrors is still in existence and now works all over the City of Sudbury.

Within a year, we had taken over and re-opened many other spaces throughout the neighbourhood. The closed-down St. Gabriel School became our office and the centre of Myths and Mirrors, the francophone programs and the Aboriginal program. After endless meetings, education of local bureaucrats and pressure tactics, we got access to a unit in each of the public housing projects in the neighbourhood for mums and tots programs. We got the neglected basement of a church in another end of the neighbourhood for an after-school program. We had a cooperative games program called Peaceful Playgrounds going in most of the neighbourhood schools. Our community workers met with families, did crisis intervention and helped them advocate with the agencies and with governments for the services they needed. We even ran an Aboriginal family camp for a few years.

Regular community meetings were held to decide what we would work on next. We incorporated, and a governance council was formed out of the original planning committee. The caucuses were retained. An annual meeting (with a feast) reported to the community on what we were doing so far. Weekly staff meetings provided cohesion and an opportunity to generate new ideas and discard those that weren't working. We quickly had over twenty-five staff — almost all part-time, some working split shifts to staff all the different programs. The quick growth of staff from the neighbourhood helped us identify leadership and support it.

We also wanted to heal the devastated local environment. The Urban Issues Program of the Bronfman Foundation provided funding to hire a project naturalist, whose job was to create an interest in environmental protection in the community. Clem Farmer led the work on the O'Connor Park redesign and then took on the Save the Mountain campaign. The hill in the middle of the neighbourhood, which the children called the Mountain, had been identified in our workshop with Paul Hogan as the key to the neighbourhood's character. A few years after Better Beginnings started, a plan emerged from the city to build housing on it. The neighbourhood was outraged — this was their wild spot. Everyone had stories about playing on the Mountain. We decided to undertake a campaign to save it as a natural heritage area.

Myths and Mirrors began a number of ritualized celebrations related to the Mountain with puppets and art. Community residents collected stories of how people had used the Mountain in the past and brought them to City Council. We circulated a petition. We even found a famous architect to argue on our behalf. Aboriginal ceremonies and prayers were held there. We won. A small circle garden was built at the foot of the Mountain by the children to commemorate the events and give thanks.

Our project naturalist was able to bring ideas from other parts of the world into our neighbourhood and share them with the children and families: we had a yellow-fish road program; we cleaned up Junction Creek and sampled for contaminants; we developed a schoolyard garden program and a community garden program at the housing projects; we planted trees and re-greened the neighbourhood. Many years later, those trees have grown to provide shade and beauty in places where only ugliness was before.

Our neighbourhood was and continues to be impoverished, and we wanted to take on some of the material issues facing us, like food and shelter. We organized GEODE, Grassroots Economic Organization Development and Evaluation, to do this.

GEODE used ideas from all around the world to build a program. We brought in films and speakers to tell us about what had been done in other communities. We set up a collective kitchen after a visit from an organizer from Peru. We set up a Good Food Box and Community Shared Agriculture. GEODE purchased a community van to get people around, as the public transportation systems were so useless. It set up micro-enterprise borrowers circles and tried to get funding for a community loan fund. GEODE worked with EcoAction Sudbury and the non-profit housing sector to advocate for city-wide programs for more housing and energy conservation programs. Better Beginnings now has a Community Closet, providing clothing, books and small appliances for the neighbourhood. The collective kitchens, where people learned to cook together, are now run by the Aboriginal Health Centre. EcoAction's energy program has been absorbed by the municipality.

Always at the heart of what we did were the children. New programs were initiated by the federal government, and Better Beginnings was able to bring them to the neighbourhood: the Aboriginal Hub, Baby's Breath, new early childhood programs. Pre-teen programs became increasingly important as the project went along, and we did everything we could to provide them — from Myths and Mirrors' Better B Girls, to a pre-teen program at O'Connor Park. We advocated (successfully) with the schools to get Ojibwe language programs.

In 1995, Mike Harris and the "Common Sense Revolution" took over the provincial government. This was also the year that the core provincial funding for Better Beginnings had to be renewed. Although we in Sudbury had been able to get project funding from other sources for the pre-teen programs, a part-time staff for Myths and Mirrors, the project naturalist and GEODE, we were totally dependent on the province for the core programs. As Mike the Knife started slashing, the first thing he did was cut welfare by 21.6 percent. The people in the neighbourhood were in shock. They were already impoverished, and this was too much.

At Sudbury Better Beginnings, we were afraid to advocate, because we knew it would mean that our core provincial funding would be cut. Our council immediately called a retreat to talk about what to do. We agreed to increase food in all programs and make sure our community workers were ready for crisis interventions for those most stressed out. But we also wanted to fight the cuts; we used our base in the neighbourhoods to organize two groups unaffiliated with the project itself: the Sudbury Social Justice Coalition and the Bleeding Hearts Coalition (in response to Tory jibes about "bleeding heart liberals").

The Social Justice Coalition organized vigils and demonstrations and sent petitions to Toronto. It individually advocated for people in crisis. The Bleeding Heart Coalition was made up of agency representatives and did roughly the same thing, but represented professionals.

With others, the Social Justice Coalition organized the Celebration of Resistance, a march of labour, community organizations and Aboriginal groups to affirm that Sudbury did not support the cuts and mean-spirited politics of the provincial Tories. It was our contribution to the Ontario-wide Labour Days of Action going on at that time.

The Celebration was organized through mass, consensus-based meetings with all the players. This was not easy in a town where labour is so used to being in charge. We wanted to ensure that Aboriginal people and the victims of Harris's cuts organized the event and had ownership of it. The older labour activists rejected consensus and didn't see the need to involve all the other "weirdos." They wanted the event to consist of a lot of militant speeches and a big parade. The Ontario Federation of Labour sent in a professional organizer to tell us what to do; we were insulted and concerned that he would wreck the spirit we had been building in the community. We had to organize and assert our own methods of working together, which differed dramatically from the usual labour union methods.

The Sudbury Celebration of Resistance — our Day of Action — was probably unique to the province. It started with a sunrise ceremony on the Mountain, had a 6000 strong demonstration through the streets with giant puppets, with representation from almost every community group and interest, and ended with a rally at the arena.

In the end, our provincial funding was not cut, and we continued as before. Our members continued to advocate. Local people worked with agencies to strengthen their stories, change schools and support local health centres. In 2003, neighbourhood leaders helped organize "Justice with Dignity" around the death of Kimberley Rogers, who had been convicted of welfare fraud, and sentenced to house arrest.

We could not have done it without the provincial money, but we spent a lot of time and energy preparing reports and spinning the project to fit parameters laid down by the funders, energy going to the care and feeding of funders and political allies. Although we were able to spread out sources of funding — Bronfman, Sudbury Community Foundation, Evergreen Foundation and the federal government — and house some programs with other organizations, Better Beginnings remains dependent on provincial core funding.

Although Harris cut back the research component of the project, the baseline data on the children was still in place. In 2004 a number of the researchers received funding to analyze the three sites with programs for four to eight year olds. To no one's surprise, they found that the program worked even by traditional economic standards; it was saving the province $938 per year per child. Better Beginnings Better Futures sites saved costs in visits to a family physician, grade repetition, special education, arrests, social welfare assistance and the disability support program. The study also found significant statistical differences between Better Beginnings kids and the comparison site.[4] So, the project is a success, not only in community terms, but in the measurable terms of the research.

The Donovan-Flour Mill neighbourhood has not been gentrified, and it still faces the continuous onslaught of deepening impoverishment, displacement and cutbacks in education and public services that other neighbourhoods face. Still a visit to the area today finds many oases of peace, kindness and sharing, grassroots leaders who know what the people are facing and a democratic way of working that inspires other agencies and organizations.

Most of the local staff we hired originally still work there, and the leaders we developed inspire the rest of the city and — in fact — the country, with what they have learned.

Notes

1. For a good description of the function of "conjunctural moments," see Deborah Barndt, *Naming the Moment* (Toronto: Between the Lines, 1989).
2. A film interview with Paul Hogan can be found at <http://sunsite.queensu.ca/memorypalace/garden/spiralgarden/index.html>.
3. Myths and Mirrors website <http://mythsandmirrors.wordpress.com/>.
4. The provincial Better Beginnings website <http://bbbf.queensu.ca/pdfs/Grade%2012%20report%20FINAL%20version.pdf> "Grade 12 Final Report" p. 13:
   - Academic functioning: the percentage of young people using Special Education was 19 percent at the Better Beginnings sites and 27 percent at the comparison site.
   - Teachers reported hyperactivity/inattentiveness among the children was 4.3 percent at Better Beginnings sites and 5.7 percent at the comparison site;
   - Parents reporting "healthy family functioning" was 23.7 percent at Better Beginnings sites but only 22.9 percent at the comparison site;
   - Good parent social supports were acknowledged by 21.22 percent of parents at Better Beginnings sites and only by 20.1 percent at the comparison site;
   - Neighbourhood satisfaction was 21.7 percent at Better Beginnings and 19.6 percent at the comparison site.

4

Transforming Our Culture

> You are members of a generation which inherits a diminished earth; degraded air and water and soil and sunshine. Wind, water, earth and fire, the basic supports for life, are all badly damaged. If you carry on with the life-style and philosophy of your parents and grandparents your children will inherit an uninhabitable earth. You must live lives radically different from the lives they lived. Your principal problem is to defend the earth from further damage and to inaugurate the great healing of the earth that is so essential.... the culture is brainsick as well as soul-sick.... The culture made it OK to destroy the source of life, to lay waste that which the human cannot do without. A culture which allows its top soil to be washed away and blown away and paved over can only be called sick.... Its thinking apparatus is diseased.[1]

In my early years as an activist, I would have argued that we must start making change by organizing around environmental, economic or political questions. I no longer believe that is how to do it. Unless we consciously resist it, our practice will be shaped by the destructive corporate paradigm of "power-over." To free ourselves from the systems that hold power, we have to build a culture of hope. And that begins in our own lives and the lives of our neighbours and friends. It's like gardening: if we want strong, beautiful and healthy plants, we have to build up the soil.

Many pressures work to disorganize our community-building efforts, or confine our efforts to a small group of friends, or make our efforts backfire with bullying, racism and sexism. Unless our ideas and practice create enthusiasm in volunteers and underpaid staff, we go nowhere.

Our lives seem to be constantly rushed and messed up: our work lives are unfulfilling, and if we stop to think about it are often downright damaging to other people. Our children seem to be growing up in a world full of fear, bad values and chaos. What we really battle when we face our powerlessness is *despair*. Asking ourselves and others to take on the work of confronting these systems of domination is asking people to take on a dangerous and difficult task.

Our education system has produced little in the way of critical conscious-ness. Working-class children are systematically humiliated and made to feel inadequate in a system that devalues their own experience and teaches them they are failures. This has become scandalous as class size increases and teachers' organizations are undermined. Illiteracy even among high school students is growing rapidly. A 2006 report from Statistics Canada found that 42 percent of Canadians were semi-literate (having skills below the internationally accepted standard of literacy required to cope in a modern society); 15 percent of these cannot read the writing on an aspirin bottle, and 27 percent can't read ordinary hazard warnings.[2]

The fact is that for a lot of kids — working class, poor, disabled, Aboriginal, immigrant — the school system is a place where you learn to hide what you don't know from the teacher and the other students and where you only preserve your dignity and self-respect by rebellion. Unfortunately, many kids rebel not only against the school system but against knowledge and book learning.[3] We all have fragile egos and lots of pride. Scars left from the education system prevent us from learning as adults; they interfere with our ability to say "I don't know"; they destroy confidence that would enable people to organize together for change.

Most of us find it easier to learn and to take risks when we can do it with other people we trust. When we don't feel comfortable with others, we spend our time and energy strategizing to protect ourselves from failure or being rejected or looking foolish. Learning to work with others and build community is a skilled trade.

Community-building is an important force in our struggle to save the earth from ecological destruction, nuclear war and human misery. We have to take its power very seriously. In her novel *The Bean Trees*, Barbara Kingsolver's main character, Taylor Greer, discovers the secret of the gorgeous wisteria vines (the bean trees) she has been admiring in Roosevelt Park:

> But this is the most interesting part: wisteria vines, like other legumes, often thrive in poor soil, the book said. Their secret is something called rhizobia. These are microscopic bugs that live underground in little knots on the roots. They suck nitrogen gas right out of the soils and turn it into fertilizer for the plant…. There's a whole invisible system for helping out the plant that you'd never guess was there.[4]

I am teaching community development to a class of twelve students from reserves in northern Ontario. One morning, they are presenting the "maps" they have made of their communities. The maps look at the cultural, social, political and economic realities of each community. As each reserve is discussed, it becomes clear that in those communities where traditional ways of life are now being practised by the leadership, the social, political and economic life of the community is also improved. Some of these reserves have managed to achieve 80 percent or more sobriety. There are interesting social programs for the young people. Women are more active in the life of the community. Disease, violence and accidents are dramatically lower. And activities to reclaim the economy and struggles around sovereignty issues are underway.

For years, Indigenous people found themselves overwhelmed by despair in their attempts to bring change to their own communities. Their subjugation had been brought about by disease, by police and army interventions, by the removal of the children to residential schools, by the forced removal of peoples for hydro dams, mines and urban development, by the imposition of regulations and laws outlawing traditional sources of income, by the plunder of their lands and resources by corporate interests and by the outlawing of their traditional language, religion and way of life. Aboriginal people found that this disempowerment was reflected in the lifestyles and social relations of their communities. Dependence on alcohol, horizontal violence and suicide were the most prevalent symptoms. To heal the circle of life meant reawakening their connection with the earth, understanding colonization and beginning once again to draw strength from traditional lifeways — returning to "the original teachings." Time and again, Indigenous people have found that the use of the medicine wheel, drum, sweat lodge and sacred pipe has the power to heal whole communities. If we are to help create communities where life can be sustained, then non-Indigenous people also have to undertake a radical transformation of our culture. We need to create learning and working environments where people feel safe enough to make these changes.

Over centuries the earth-centred way of life in Europe was destroyed through the cumulative effects of the conquests by the Romans and Christians; the destruction of ancient forests and the lives of forest-dwellers for wars and industry; the burning of the witches during the period that the European empires were plundering the rest of the world; and the lure of the growing cities. Parts of the women's movement are now "re-membering" the wisdom of the peasant wise women and forest-dwellers. Ritual and culture that are tied to ancient earth-centred practices are becoming more common in Canada.

This life-way is practical and based in what Ojibwe people call The Seven Grandfather Teachings: respect, humility, honesty, kindness, courage, sharing and strength. It cares for the earth and other human beings in ways that are just, participatory and sustainable. Discussions of these practices in North America can be found in the work of Starhawk and Joanna Macy, author of *The Work That Reconnects*,[5] the films and workshops of Velcrow Ripper[6] and the writing of Derrick Jensen,[7] to name a few.

Many of the mass protests against globalization are sustained by this kind of culture, as is the resistance of environmentalists and Aboriginal people to mines, oil sands, clear-cut logging, corporate agriculture and dragnet fishing. Even within the mainstream churches, the influence of Indigenous traditions and pressures from the feminist movement have opened liturgy and ritual to new forms and energy.

How Do We Create a Culture of Hope?

In the culture of commodities and violence, it can be hard to be creative or to have real fun. Most Euro-Canadians are taught that adult behaviour is humourless and "responsible." In activist groups we tend to be overwhelmed by how awful things are and to trudge drearily through life and our meetings; we can become bitter and angry. But we do not have to spend all our time dwelling on how bad things are. We do need to retain our courage, love of life and sense of humour. In my experience, people really want to laugh and to play with one another. Every time I'm going to try a playful exercise with a group, I'm worried that it won't succeed. It always does, and the effect it has on participants is to make them more relaxed, creative and committed in their strategic planning.

In the 1980s, the Neighbourhood Action Project in Sudbury hired five people with a long history of activism to do neighbourhood organizing in an impoverished part of the city. These people looked for ways to stimulate new ideas and community. They organized a popular theatre troop; they took workshops on how to be clowns and the clowns were suddenly everywhere; they put out a little newsletter that celebrated the victories of ordinary folk in the area; and they insisted that all of us take time to play together and laugh. The energy they generated amongst people in the neighbourhood made all sorts of other tough things possible. Their learnings are published in a little booklet called *Neighbourhood Action: Recipes for Change.*[8]

After the project, we integrated these ideas into workshops and conferences, introducing physical movement, drawing and music. A tough working session would end with a cooperative game or playing charades. We learned to do everything we could to keep all the participants involved and thinking all the time.

Now our organizations take time to plan social and cultural events — potluck suppers, picnics and dances — where people can actually play with one another. They are events for the whole family that include making up songs or playing silly games or doing dances in a round. We have found that when we don't organize in this way, some people start bickering with each other and a lot of others vote with their feet. Our strategies include activities that are outside the experience of the bureaucrats and corporate types we have to deal with: masks, clowns, physical work parties, parades, guerrilla

44

theatre and so on. For the members of our groups, we introduced rituals: opportunities to notice and to mark the seasons and the phases of the moon; ways to connect with the power and sanity of the earth herself.

In the summer of 1989, I had the honour to be part of a gathering of Aboriginal people on an island in Georgian Bay. The occasion was the making of a film, entitled *Get Real or Get Lost: The Original Peoples Speak to the Human Family*, by a group of German film-makers.[9] The gathering was organized by Anishinaabe elder Art Solomon to provide a setting for elders to share the prophecies and for people to spend a week living and working together outdoors. One evening we sat around the fire under the stars while Art made a drum for Leonard Peltier, and stories were shared from the past and prophecies for the future: the Hopi Prophecy, the story of the Seventh Fire and so on. This is as close as I get to understanding the power of the "sacred," not as something separate from our daily lives but as an intrinsic part of it.

For many years in Sudbury, a few of my friends and I took time to mark the turning of the seasons with small and unpretentious rituals, usually structured so that they wouldn't embarrass our children. At the winter solstice, for example, we went into the woods and tobogganed and played in the snow. We built a fire and burned symbols of those things we wanted to end in our lives in the coming year and buried symbols of those things we want to grow. We ate hotdogs and drank hot chocolate. For all of us, this was really Christmas, the time when light returns after the longest night of the year.

Over my years as an organizer, I have come to value the role that synchronicity plays in the work. It takes many forms. Sometimes, weather creates a moment; sometimes, a chance meeting or unexpected relationship; sometimes a dream; sometimes an animal shows itself to me. When I am doing what I am supposed to do in my life, there is support — what I need for the work — made available to me. I don't understand this, and I don't expect I ever will, but I am grateful that this Mystery is there and that it occasionally reveals itself to me when I least expect it.

Creating a Safe Learning Environment

Although there is only one reality, we all look at it through different windows. Creating an environment in which we can look through each other's windows helps us to see and act more holistically. Most formal education situations give value only to the teacher's experience and devalue the perceptions and life experience of the learners. Since most teachers come from the privileged classes in society, what is taught is the perspective of the privileged. "Popular education" turns this process upsidedown and starts with the experience of the participants.

In our society, control of information goes beyond the concentrated ownership of internet, newspaper and television chains to the question of the language and forms in which information is kept and exchanged.[10] In Canada, most formal knowledge is held by corporations and academics. This information and analysis is important for community folk to know, but even if we get access, we may not understand it. Knowledge is divided into disciplines and specialties with their own vocabulary and jargon. The descriptions of the same forest by an economist, a biologist, a risk assessor, a lumber company, a logger and a First Nations person would sound completely different, but in fact they are all important to understanding that forest and what needs to be done to protect it.

These different languages are related to socio-economic class and bring with them certain privileges. Ethnic accents, grammatical differences and size of vocabulary are instant indicators of one's position in society. It is difficult to imagine a person who has been trained to think and talk like a bank president having to argue with a welfare administrator over their cheque. Conversely, it is almost impossible to imagine someone who talks like a Toronto street kid running a bank.

Real learning involves some risks, because it challenges people to change their roles in society. We have found that some situations are more conducive to learning and participation than others. The following conditions may create an environment where people are ready to risk and learn with one another:

- getting past the roles we create for ourselves or that are created for us; being more than "the professional," "the welfare recipient," "the victim";
- feeling that our ideas are equally valid with everyone else's and that we won't be dismissed or laughed at if we are shown to be wrong;
- getting past private property in ideas. Not feeling that because we said the idea, we have to defend it to the death or our personhood is at stake;
- having the totality of our lives present at the meeting; taking time to care for one another as people with full agendas and concerns outside the meeting;
- equality and willingness to give to one another in need. So, for example, if I tell you that I need material help, you will share with me; or if I tell you I need time, you will find it for me;
- opening up our spirit of creativity and play, getting away from verbal knowledge. Too much of our activity is ruled by articulate people. We need the wisdom and experience of people who express themselves differently. When we take time to work in clay together, or to cook together, or to draw, we develop new lines of trust and communication;

- being able to confront and deal with issues of racism, sexism and ho-mophobia. These never go away because we ignore them, they only get worse;
- working together on a common project. There is nothing like "doing" together to learn to work together. The sooner the better;
- developing activities together that increase economic and political terms security for group members. A group that helps me gain a living or have political power will get more of my allegiance in terms of time and energy than one that is purely social;
- doing something of great significance. It will attract more energy. We all want to be part of making history if we only knew how; and
- celebrating our achievements and our heroes. When we do something good, we need people to acknowledge it publicly.

Popular Education: Learner-Centred Learning

The term "popular education" is attributed to Paulo Friere, a Brazilian educator who developed and popularized the methodology. His most well-known book is *Pedagogy of the Oppressed*. Popular education is education for empowerment. It brings people together so that they can be better equipped to change the world. It asks them to decide what they want to learn and what is relevant to their lives, and helps them organize with one another. It moves through five distinct phases: the participant's own experience, naming the experience, analysis of the experience (perhaps with inputs from people outside their experience), planning action to be taken from this learning and doing.[11] The website of Popular Education News has a number of excellent resources for popular education methods.

Consciousness-Raising: Talking in Protected Space

Consciousness-raising was the foundation on which the women's movement was built. Groups of women would get together regularly and "talk bitter-ness," which would reveal to one another the truth of their lives. Sometimes, we became very angry, sometimes we cried, or laughed. It was freeing and wonderful to finally be able to tell the truth as we experienced it. From the small beginnings of these groups grew movements that have re-shaped history. As one woman at that time said to me: "Now I know the real meaning of 'ig-norance is bliss.' I can't ever go back now that I know what's happening."

Each group had certain rules. Women spoke in protected space: they were not interrupted while they told their story. What went on in the group was private to that group. No subject was taboo, and we accepted one an-other and our struggles to free ourselves from our conditioning. We need to continue this practice.

In Indigenous communities, people use the "healing circle" to accomplish similar ends. In one form of the practice, squares of felt bearing the sacred colours are passed around the circle, and each person talks about how the gifts of those colours are working in their life at that time, both the positive and the negative. The space is also "protected" as people talk.

Using some techniques from consciousness-raising at the beginning of a meeting can also ensure that we bring our whole selves to a meeting. This shifts the energy of the meeting and enables authentic relationships to develop between participants. There are methods for starting a group meeting that enable participants to feel safe to speak up and relate to each other as whole people. One example is "circling in" — giving each participant a few minutes to say how they are doing before the meeting starts. Another way is to use an exercise like The Web of Influences.

Exercise: The Web of Influences

Divide people into groups of five (make sure they don't just sit with their friends) and ask them to take a few minutes to draw a picture of the influences in their life at this time: historical/cultural, social/emotional, physical/economic and political/mental. Have individual worksheets prepared ahead of time with a circle divided into four quadrants to work on. When the individual pictures are finished, the small group members discuss with each other which influences create hope and energy in their lives and which influences drain them. It is always effective. When people do this or something similar at the beginning of a meeting, someone usually says later, "I don't know why we had to do that exercise, but there sure are a lot of diverse and interesting people at this meeting." The truth is, they would never have discovered the diversity of the participants if they hadn't taken the time to find out.

We can also do a similar exercise using clay. Participants sit in small groups; each one is given a piece of clay or play-dough to work with. Ask them to meditate on their fears for the meeting and shape the clay as they think. When they are done, they place the clay in front of them, and then describe to the others in the group what the shape means. Then ask participants to shape their clay figure into a form that represents the strengths they bring to the gathering, and discuss this. At the end, the figures are put in the centre of the circle, and participants name their strengths the whole group.

Building Visions

If we don't like the way the world is now, then we need to understand what a healthy society would look like. If we are going to spend our lives working for change, we need a vision worth giving our life for.

Over the years, I have led many different groups in vision exercises. On most occasions they were energizing and exciting activities. On one occasion, it created a lot of tension and anxiety — when some middle-class church folk were working with a number of leaders of anti-poverty groups. For the impoverished people at that gathering, talking about their dreams in front of comfortable church folk was just too difficult and painful. Be sensitive about when and how these exercises are used.

Visioning can be as simple as asking participants to sit in small groups of five to seven people they are comfortable with and imagine that they could redesign their community in a very basic way. Ask them to choose some of the questions below to explore with each other and then discuss their findings with the larger group. They could also answer the questions by making murals or collages. They will probably find that the small groups agree with each other in most of the answers.

- What is our relationship to the natural world? How do we ensure that the environment is protected?
- How do people get food? What do they eat? How is it distributed? How is it produced?
- Where do we get fuel and energy?
- How do we handle the waste products created by our consumption?
- How are people sheltered? How do they live with one another? Of what materials are their shelters built? What do we do about the old-style buildings? What are the sources of heat and light?
- How are children educated? What do they learn?
- How do we care for children, the infirm and the elderly?
- How are decisions made? Do some people control others? How are deviants or violent persons dealt with?
- How do people travel?
- How do people get and share information?

Visions are born out of struggle; they will change and shift as people work for change. None of us know what the world will be like in fifty years. It will be a product of our work for cooperative, just and earth-centered ways of living as much as it will be a product of the continuing attempts for control by the power structures.

Activist Theatre

Live theatre can be used effectively to create new culture and to involve the community. In the past thirty years, many groups have explored the use of theatre, giant puppets, body sculpture, guerrilla theatre and other techniques to organize.

While theatre and social movements differ in their methods and specific goals, they do have a common concern — opening space in public forums for people whose voices often go unheard. For theatre artists who engage in activism, a common concern is an exploration of the ways in which the formal qualities of their art form allow them to create discussion about the ways in which important social issues affect the everyday lives of people.[12]

Essentially, collective theatre is a tool that brings people together and uses games and other techniques to help them relax with one another; they work on the development of a script out of their own realities. The script is agreed upon by the whole group; they learn the parts and perform it. Sometimes these groups work with professional theatre people, sometimes they just do it on their own. If they have the opportunity to work with professionals, they can learn new skills in the process. However, if the professionals do not respect the knowledge and experience of the participants, the exercise can do more harm than good.

Myths and Mirrors and other theatre activists around the world have been inspired by the work of Brazilian Augusto Boal, the father of "theatre of the oppressed."[13] In the 1980 and 1990s, he conducted numerous workshops in the method in North America and Europe. Boal said: "While some people make theatre, we all are theatre." He created theatre workshops and performances to engage people in interaction, dialogue, critical thinking and fun. The workshops have two basic activities:

- *Games*: The games serve to heighten our senses and to break our habitual behaviour. Many of the games involve real interaction with other participants, developing trust and having a good time.
- *Structured exercises with real content*: image theatre, forum theatre, cop-in-the-head, image theatre, rainbow of desire are just a few of the structured exercises.

Doug Patterson describes a couple of these exercises:

> Image Theatre uses the human body as a tool of representing feelings, ideas, and relationships. Through sculpting others or using our own body to demonstrate a body position, participants create anything from one-person to large-group image sculptures that reflect the sculptor's impression of a situation or oppression.
>
> Forum Theatre works from rehearsal improvisation to create a scene of a specific oppression. Using the Greek terms "protagonist" and "antagonist," Forum Theatre seeks to show a person (the protagonist) who is trying to deal with an oppression and failing

because of the resistance of one or more obstacles (the antagonists). Forum scenes can be virtual one-act plays or more often short scenes. In either case, a full presentation is offered to the audience. The joker (difficultator) then says to the audience we will do this again, and if you would do something different than what the protagonist (not the antagonists) is doing, stand up and yell stop. The protagonist will then sit down and the audience member is invited forward to show their solution of the moment. Once the intervention is performed, the audience invariably applauds, and the joker invites the audience to discuss the proposed solution, and to offer even more solutions.[14]

In Winnipeg, the No Name Brand Clan, a project of the Manitoba Popular Theatre Alliance from 1986 to 1990, arose from the collective experience of single mums on social assistance. They used Boal techniques[15] to write and perform plays that helped people understand and engage in their issues. In Sudbury, the Better B Girls were pre-teens who collectively developed performances using Boal techniques to examine problems in their lives. In Vancouver, Headlines Theatre creates many interactive forum theatre projects, and their work generated a community action report.

Other theatrical activities integrate public art, collective creation and fierce imagination. In Vancouver, the Public Dreams Society creates rituals to mark the turning of the year that bring thousands of people together in a celebration of the natural world. Theatre companies like Rising Tide reflect back to the community the possibilities for change in their lives. Native Earth Performing Arts and De-ba-jeh-mu-jig Theatre Group use the Aboriginal worldview to create brilliant plays and to reinterpret European classics like Julius Caesar.

Speaking Truth

Public opinion and what is acceptable to the public are manipulated by media images and slogans. The phrase "right to life" has come to mean being against abortion. "Democracy" is taken to be the same thing as capitalism. The stereotypes called up by words like "feminist," "anarchist" and "environmentalist" are all negative for large parts of the population. Calling someone a "terrorist," like calling someone a "communist," is a show-stopper.

Community groups also have to learn how to shape public opinion. We need to use images and slogans — "messaging" — to speak truth: to reclaim this territory for the culture of hope. We need to have our own public relations campaigns for what we stand for and what we do. Our public image is important, but it doesn't have to be a phony one. As a group, we can choose the image we want to project and then look for opportunities to develop it.

When the group End Legislated Poverty was looking for a way to raise the issue of poverty in British Columbia at a time when the media generally appeared to have little interest, they decided to focus on a school lunch program for children, because it would have more media appeal. It worked. "Poor kids" were important; "low income parents" weren't.

Robbie Gordon's useful book, *We Interrupt This Program: A Citizen's Guide to Using the Media for Social Change*, states:

> How the media reacts to your group and its concerns rests largely on how much you've thought through your media efforts — how steady an eye you can keep on your goals — and at the same time, how well you understand and respect the role, function and purpose of the media (even though, sometimes, it appears as though the media does not really understand or respect its own role, function and purpose). If, for example, one of your overall goals is to get fair coverage of your group's action, you will need to spend a number of months laying the groundwork: slowly building good personal relations with reporters and assignment editors, establishing credibility, reliability and a reputation for being concerned, honest and interested in the public good. Prepare extensive press packets with adequate information for reporters, being sure reporters get enough information and get an interview with the necessary persons. Releasing information to certain sources could also help those relations.[16]

Too often our groups don't understand that what is important to us may not be news to the media. Success in using the media depends on our ability to translate our group's information and activities into news. What are the characteristics of *news*? *Making the News: A Guide to Using the Media* points out that all news stories have to have at least some of the following elements: conflict, immediacy, novelty, peril, locality, human interest. The story has to have some "hook" in it that makes it appear sensational. Generally, the media will not report ongoing activities or situations, unless they can focus on a particular person or event. Creating these events is one way to get and hold their attention.[17]

For example, groups have held attention on the housing issue in their neighbourhood with stories of individual problems and victories, with demonstrations, pickets and parades. Often the media find demonstrations and pickets boring, unless we give them a "photo opportunity": dress up a pet, give a child a sign, make a presentation, use a huge banner. At one point in Sudbury we called attention to the need for emergency shelter by inviting the media to the official opening of The Tom Davies Emergency Shelter for

Families (Davies was chair of the Regional Municipality of Sudbury). The "shelter" was a cardboard shack we had thrown up overnight at a major intersection, where we served bannock and hot chocolate.

Anti-globalization protests have shown the power of internet organizing. Using social networking sites like Facebook and YouTube, the movement has been able to contact potential participants, select its own slogans and images, and successfully counter the propaganda surrounding elite economic summits. (If we do use Facebook and other social networking sites, we should be aware that they have a scary data-collection function that can be used to target activists.)

Our Own Media

The Innu pioneered the use of the internet during their struggles against NATO low-level flying, the Churchill Falls Hydro Project and the Voisey's Bay nickel mine in the early 1990s. Their website <innu.ca> caught the imagination of people around the world with stories, photos and analyses of their struggles.

Kitchenuhmaykoosib Inninuwug (KI) in northern Ontario used this medium brilliantly in defending their land from a junior mining company in the late 2000s. Throughout their struggle, their website carried messages from the chief and supporters, as well as photos and videos of actions. Two blogs from community activists were effective in providing analyses of the struggle. Since KI is a fly-in community, access to wireless internet enabled them to engage with environmental and social justice groups and to remain in charge of the process. When their leadership was jailed for six months, they were able to use the internet while in jail to maintain contact with their community.

This was possible because of the development of Aboriginal service provider K-Net in the late 1990s. K-Net is based in Sioux Lookout in northwestern Ontario and services approximately fifty Cree communities in the region. Almost all of them are fly-in communities, except when the winter roads are open. A small group of technically savvy activists from the communities negotiated with government funders to set up a high-speed internet service across the territory, which includes telemedicine, computers in the schools and email service.[18]

There are times when we need to consider creating our own media to get information across. Many community groups have their own websites and listserves, have started their own newspapers, made their own DVDs, videos and slide shows, and done community theatre. Such activities can have the added advantage of training local people in a variety of new skills.

In Canada, The Dominion, rabble.ca and straightgoods.com provide alternative sources of news and analysis, and all are available online. Key to the success of any website are effective strategies to drive people to it. The use of twitter, social networking and diligent use of key words in articles are all strategies that work. Reporters Without Borders has written a *Handbook for Bloggers and Cyberdissidents*:

> The handbook offers practical advice and techniques on how to create a blog, make entries and get the blog to show up in search engine results. It gives clear explanations about blogging for all those whose online freedom of expression is subject to restrictions, and it shows how to sidestep the censorship measures imposed by certain governments, with a practical example that demonstrates the use of the censorship circumvention software Tor.[19]

DVDs and Videos

Getting members of a community involved in making a video about themselves and their issue can be a wonderful project, even if no one except the local neighbourhood sees the final product. People love the opportunity to talk for a camera and to analyze their community together. A community meeting later to review the results can get diverse groups really discussing the issues. Everyone will come. In Sioux Lookout, Ontario, a video about the industrial and racial shifts in the community was used to focus a community development strategy. A video about a community garden in Regent Park in Toronto created a number of local heroes. Videos made from presentations and workshops can also extend their useful life considerably.

The equipment available to us (through unions, community cable channels, schools and churches) is rarely good quality, although it is increasingly inexpensive. As a result, the finished product is not often good enough to be shown on television, but it can go on YouTube. Effective videos are a lot of work and do require some skills in filming, scripting, editing and organizing. Help in making them may be available from local community colleges or community channels.

In Newfoundland, years ago, Memorial University Extension Department ran one of the most exciting community television experiments in Canada. They had a portable transmitter on the back of a truck that they took to different communities. They would stay in a community for five days. Each day at about four o'clock, a village could tune in to films about their part of the island. High school students interspersed the film with announcements. In the evening there would be a panel discussion and then there would be phone-in questions for the panel. The last part of each show was live local entertainment. The low-power transmitter used in this way was a valuable tool for community analysis and education.

As Arundhati Roy says:

> Our strategy should be not only to confront empire but to lay siege to it. To deprive it of oxygen. To shame it. To mock it. With our art, our music, our literature, our stubbornness, our joy, our brilliance, our sheer relentlessness…. The corporate revolution will collapse if we refuse to buy what they are selling — their ideas, their version of history, their wars, their weapons and their notion of inevitability. Remember this. We be many and they be few. They need us more than we need them. Another world is not only possible, she is on her way. On a quiet day, I can hear her breathing.[20]

Notes

1. James Berry, "Circular #110," *The Center for Reflection on the Second Law,* 1989 <crfsl.org>.
2. Dan Bjarnson, "Canada's Shame" *CBC*-The National, May 24, 2006.
3. George Martel, *The Politics of the Canadian Public School* (Toronto: James, Lewis and Samue, l1972).
4. Barbara Kingsolver, *The Bean Trees* (New York: Harper Perennial, 1988), p. 227.
5. Joanna Macy, *The Work That Reconnects* (Gabriola Island, BC: New Society Publishers, 2006).
6. Velcrow Ripper, *Fierce Light: When Spirit Meets Action.* Seville Pictures in co-production with the National Film Board of Canada, 2008 <www.fiercelight.org>.
7. <Derrickjensen.org>.
8. Neighbourhood Action Project and Sticks and Stones, *Neighbourhood Action: Recipes for Change* (Sudbury, 1983).
9. Pierre Hoffman, *Get Real or Get Lost: The Original Peoples Speak to the Human Family.* ZDF + WDR, (Bern, Germany: One World Film, 1989).
10. I am particularly indebted to Dr. Dorothy Smith of the Ontario Institute for Studies in Education for her insights in this area, which she shared with me through numerous conversations.
11. Rick Arnold, Deborah Barndt and Bev Burke, *A New Weave: Popular Education in Canada and Central America* (Toronto: CUSO Development Education and Ontario Institute for Studies in Education, 1986).
12. Uzma Mazhar, "Theatrics: Theatre Activism, for Women, by Women," March 8, 2009 <http://archives.dawn.com/weekly/images/images1.htm>.
13. Augusto Boal, *Games for Actors and Non-Actors* (New York: Routledge, 1992).
14. Douglas L. Paterson, *Theatre of the Oppressed Workshops,* 1995 <http://www.wwcd.org/action/Boal.html>.
15. Povnet website <http://www.povnet.org/node/3529>.
16. Robbie Gordon, *We Interrupt This Program: A Citizen's Guide to Using the Media* (Amherst: University of Massachusetts, 1978) p. 13.
17. Michael Ura, *Making the News: A Guide to Using the Media* (Vancouver: West Coast Environmental Law Research Foundation, 1989).

18. Wendy Quarry and Ricardo Ramirez, *Communication for Another Development: Listening Before Telling* (London: Zed Books, 2009) p. 99–100.
19. Reporters Without Borders, *Handbook for Bloggers and Cyberdissidents,* 2009 <http://en.rsf.org/new-version-of-handbook-for-16-07-2009,33844.html>.
20. Arundhati Roy, Speech at the World Social Forum in Porto Alegre, Brazil, January 27, 2003, in Judy Rebick, *Transforming Power: From the Personal to the Political* (Toronto: Penguin, 2009), p. 21).

Part 3

Learning to Work Together

The Myths and Mirrors Community Arts team working together.

5

Working Together

To transform the world into something better requires organizing. We have to learn to trust each other and work together in groups. More attempts at change and community-building fail because we can't get along with one another than for any other reason. Our organizations should reflect the kind of world we want to create: cooperative, honest, caring and exciting. Because we do not have access to a lot of money, we have to depend on the enthusiasm and commitment of volunteers. Otherwise, we can go nowhere.

People get involved in and stay committed to change organizations for a variety of reasons: they share the organization's goals; they learn new things; they enjoy the company of other members; and they feel respected and liked by the other members. If the organization does not satisfy some or all these needs, they leave. If people feel their ideas and labour are essential to the group, they are more likely to stay involved. Unfortunately, we too often blindly model our groups on the structures of the dominant society. This is death for collective, participatory work. This chapter provides tools for creating alternative organizational forms.

Most neighbourhoods are not warm and fuzzy places, although they do have their moments. They have all sorts of class differences, social differences, racism and homophobia, historical feuds and bullying relationships. The way we design our cities makes it worse. In rural areas, the attempts by mining companies, oil companies and similar intruders to win a "social licence to operate" deepen divisions and encourage corruption.

Getting along with each other, when we have been trained from infancy to be competitive and individualistic, takes hard work, but gatherings and actions where people truly cooperate and work together for a common purpose can be so exciting they give me shivers. Organizing in this manner is not a mystery; it is a skilled and creative process that can be learned.

Getting Started: Leadership and the Core Group

We can start organizing with people we know. We don't have to organize people different from ourselves. We look for the place of least resistance, where our friends are talking about a problem or experiencing one. We acknowledge their worries and fears about the world around them. Some people are particularly prone to downplaying their own concerns. "So many people are worse off than me, I have no right to feel bad," is a pretty common statement.

We start by finding a core group: people who are deeply concerned about the issue but come from different parts of the community. They don't have to be the big names, but they should have leadership potential. If they bring a friend or colleague with whom they feel comfortable, they will be not isolated in the group. One group started organizing with a regular Wednesday night potluck supper for about twelve people who wanted to work together on environmental issues.

Nurturing this core group is extremely important. We need to have not only political experiences together but cultural and social ones as well. We make planning to have fun a part of our agenda together. One of the functions of the core group should be to support one another emotionally and morally. "Solidarity is based on the principle that we are willing to put ourselves at risk to protect one another."[1]

Leaders can be anyone. Si Kahn says: "Good leaders are willing to step outside themselves into people's lives."[2] Leaders are good listeners, make friends easily, are comfortable with their own ideas, work hard, don't discourage easily, ask questions and have vision and a sense of humour. They also need specific skills, but these skills can be learned, through reading, experience and apprenticeship. Leaders are not necessarily talkative people, and they frequently are not the spokespersons of an organization.

The only dangerous leadership is authoritarian or hidden, so that it does not operate with the consent of the group. We need to watch out for bullies; we are talking about building "power-with" not "power-over." Leadership is very different from authority, which carries with it the power to compel. Being a leader is not a position we design for ourselves; it is an honour given to us by the people who come to respect our judgment. There are different roles for leaders: the healer, the catalyst, the facilitator and the elder.

In traditional Indigenous culture, people of wisdom, honesty and experience were asked to be "elders," a position that carries grave responsibility for guiding the community. Elders are people chosen by their peers, and they serve without the rewards of the system. Because they listen, they are knowledgeable about the state of their community as few others are.

In the world of power-over, instead of relying on our lived experience we tend to equate leadership roles with certain occupations: lawyers, social workers, doctors, priests, successful business owners, politicians. Although these people have technical competence in their field, that does not mean they have any credentials to advise on other matters in life.

Effective community organizing means strengthening the key leaders. The following suggestions are ways to do that:

- Recognition. Let them know that they are recognized as leaders by others in the community, seek their advice, honour them. Make sure this is sincere, not just flattery.
- Information about the outside world. Provide opportunities, however informal, for them to be better educated about the national and global causes of and solutions to the problems they work with every day. Help them get on the internet.
- Information about what others do in similar situations. Set up opportunities for them to talk over situations with their peers, to share stories and ideas from their locality and from other places.
- Rest. Provide breaks and respite from their daily tasks from time to time, so they have time to reflect or to play or to learn. Maybe we can take on some of their responsibilities for them so they can attend an event.
- A chance to meet like people and be appreciated for their knowledge and strength. This does not always mean pulling them out of the local situation for conferences and workshops but could involve finding ways to provide that support where they are: bring the world to them.

It is not always easy matching leaders to a cause. They are probably busy already with important paid or unpaid work. There are many older women who won't even speak in front of their husbands and youth who won't speak in front of their parents. Many will claim they have nothing to say. Sometimes people are afraid of their neighbours and resist getting to know them. Often people will not organize for their own interests but will do it for the good of others. Putting together a project for children may entice the real leaders to come forward.

If we are really having trouble pulling a core group together, we should re-evaluate the issue or cause we are espousing. It might be more productive to join with a more popular activity and build from that base. Organizing should start where there is existing social energy.

Race and Class

Race and class differences do not go away just because we pretend they are not there. They get worse. We do not choose our parents or our ancestry. However, our race and class mean that we fall into cultural patterns and expectations that shape our behaviour even when we wish they didn't. For example, Europeans have a long history of hierarchical and highly structured government and legal systems. We can be murderous and barbaric in our relations with each other — our forebears killed more than 80 million people during the European tribal wars we call World War One and Two. Our patriarchal religions are often used to justify the most terrible kinds of violence and repression.

Culturally, Euro-Canadians are very verbal people with real difficulty listening. We move quickly. We are trained to be linear in our thinking. We are obsessive about germs, order and material security. Our religions are monotheistic, not connected to the earth. We have been taught nature is either something to be subdued or romanticized.

I am always shocked at how deeply these cultural patterns are ingrained in me. When Euro-Canadians work with people of other races, we have to be aware that these patterns can be oppressive to others; they are only cultural attributes and not universal values. When we deal with other races and classes, we have learn about ourselves over and over again. There is no quick fix, no absolution. We need to be rigorously honest with ourselves, having a sense of humour about our "white mistakes," working hard to unlearn the oppressive parts of our acculturation, sharing the worthwhile parts of our training and privilege where it is requested. And stereotypes about other races, cultures and classes are not only the property of white, middle-class folk. Other races have stereotypes about whites and each other.

Precisely because Western European culture is the predominant one in Canada, our work for change should try where ever possible to encourage, create space for and accept leadership from other racial and cultural groups. Other races and cultures are organizing themselves in the ways that they find appropriate. Euro-Canadians have a lot to learn. This does not mean glorifying the cultures of others. It does mean allowing the space and time for other cultural forms to emerge, to take leadership and power. If our goal is building a movement or a group from the bottom up, we need to take the time to do it right.

Being in Solidarity:
The North Eastern Ontario Women's Conference

A group of about fifteen Sudbury women had organized Women Helping Women in 1977, and in the fall of 1981, we were invited to Kirkland Lake for a conference put on by Health Canada about health promotion issues. A number of Aboriginal women were also invited. There was freezing rain on the way up from Sudbury to Kirkland — a distance of about 300 kilometres. Some First Nations women were in a car behind us. Although we knew each other slightly, we had never really worked together. We ended up having to crawl along on the edge of the highway one wheel on the gravel because the roads were glare ice. It took us about seven terrifying hours to get there. So we stopped quite often and talked with each other. During the conversation, the Aboriginal women told us that Health Canada was willing to give us — the white women — a grant to hold the next conference but that their request for money for a similar event had been refused. Outraged, we began strategizing together about what could be done about it.

By the time we got to Kirkland Lake, we had a plan, and our group ran around talking to the white women at the conference to get them onside. Then we stood up and said that we would not accept any Health Canada money unless they gave equal money to First Nations women for a parallel conference to be held in the same facility at the same time. The two conferences would have permeable boundaries so women could go back and forth between them and learn from each other.

The First Nations women got their money, and our conferences took place in Toronto. They brought in natural healers and herbalists and people from the Midewiwin Lodge. Ours was a progressive feminist conference. It worked. We learned from each other.

During the conference, the northeastern Ontario women caucused and decided to hold another gathering, this time to help feminist activists in the region understand how the decisions taken by multinational corporations created many of the problems we were confronting. So, in 1982, we organized the North Eastern Ontario Women's Conference in Sault Ste. Marie. We invited Aboriginal women, but only a few came to the first event. We then had a series of gatherings, one every six months, in different parts of northeastern Ontario, and participation grew. We asked the Aboriginal women we knew why they didn't come in greater numbers, and they said they didn't see themselves as feminists. Rather, their issues were sovereignty, resistance and healing the damage done to their people. We agreed that these were women's issues too. Subsequent conferences allowed space for First Nations women to lead the discussions. In 1988 — seven years later — the Aboriginal women organized the North Eastern Ontario Women's Conference and invited the rest of us. We learned a lot.

Euro-Canadians Working with Racialized and/or Impoverished People

Class and race are closely related. In Canada, most non-whites have less access to economic privilege than whites.[3] So, the following discussion provides key points for Euro-Canadians who work with racialized and/or people who are living in poverty. Class and race are not only conditions but processes: with patterns of oppression created through learned behaviours that serve those who hold power-over. For example, the form filled out by welfare applicants that requires birth-date and other personal information is a tool to "class" the individual and assert the power of the person administering the form.

Too often we turn racialized and/or impoverished people into professional victims: we only want to hear about their suffering. This is using their pain to educate ourselves. But in order to build their own struggle the oppressed need to know and celebrate their own strength, courage and success as survivors who are part of a world struggle for change. Glorifying the hard lives of racialized and/or impoverished people instead of recognizing them as equals comes from a particular kind of self-hatred that afflicts some whites. Putting people on pedestals keeps them from acting. Equality means valuing ourselves, and working in solidarity side-by-side.

Economically secure people tend to be preoccupied with their feelings, health, appearance and psychology. These are luxuries, and although all of these are concerns for low income people, they do not have the same significance for them. This does not mean that they only want to talk about social change and politics either.

Acting and speaking as though racialized and/or impoverished people are not as "developed" because they don't talk the same way that formally educated English-speakers do is both inaccurate and insulting. Their approach may have less abstract theory, more concrete images and more anger. It is likely also to be more spiritually based.

Hanging on to middle-class privilege — education, skills, money — instead of sharing the benefits with racialized and/or impoverished people replicates the relationships of hyper-individualism in our society. When whites from middle-class backgrounds speak as though hard work has brought them skills, education, possessions and position, they ignore the fact that most racialized and/or impoverished people work just as hard but do not get these rewards. In fact, the benefits middle-class white people enjoy are a result of the costs borne by the impoverished.

The success that middle-class whites attain for following the rules and being reasonable often leads them to think that these are also good strategies for racialized and/or impoverished people. In fact, most racialized and/or impoverished people can only succeed with these tactics if they have "acceptable" white, educated people to do it for them. Not having to worry about eating, being deported or knowing where the next dollar will come from enables middle-class white activists to take chances that are much more dangerous for racialized and/or impoverished people (civil disobedience, voluntary poverty, for example).

Middle-class white activists should not expect gratitude or recognition for their work to create space for racialized and/or impoverished people to take leadership in a group. Usually the people who know about the work will not be there by the time the space is actually occupied, and the role of the organizer will be (and should remain) invisible.

In mixed groups, we will hear many times about the terrible suffering that white people have inflicted on the Other. If our response is guilt and sorrow, we should not expect the racialized/impoverished people to comfort us, and should not become defensive and insist that we are "not like that." This is an occasion for healing and active listening. White folk cannot defend ourselves against charges of racism. If there is a defence, it will have to come from the racialized people who know us and our work.

Notes

1. Starhawk, *Truth or Dare* (New York: Harper and Row, 1987).
2. Si Kahn, *Organizing* (Toronto: McGraw-Hill, 1982). This is an excellent resource for community organizers. This section is strongly influenced by his work, a book filled with social analysis and detailed information from peoples' struggles in the United States.
3. See Grace-Edward Galabuzzi, *Canada's Economic Apartheid: The Social Exclusion of Racialized Groups in the New Century* (Toronto: Canadian Scholars Press, 2006), for a full discussion of this issue.

6

Understanding Groups and Organizations

Groups of people have their own personalities, internal conflicts and ways of behaving. The study of "group dynamics" started during the Second World War when the U.S. Defence Department was trying to help soldiers get along and cooperate under stressful conditions. There is however no reason not to appropriate these learnings for our own purposes. Looking at group process from different angles can provide some clues for making our own groups work better.

Group Participation

Group interaction falls into one of three patterns: a leader talking at the members (one-directional), a leader talking and the members answering (two-directional), or everyone talking to one another (multi-dimensional). The more interaction there is between all the members, the more sustained interest there is likely to be in the group. Although groups that are dominated by one or two people can be very productive in the short term, they tend to lose membership and energy over time. As an organizer, I may have a much stronger commitment to the group, or more grandiose ideas about what we should do, than the other members have. The willingness of group members to give time and energy will be determined by many factors.

A few times I have asked people in a workshop to use body sculpture to show how they felt people related to the issue we were working on. Every time, at the centre of the sculpture was a group of people actively engaged although they might be in conflict with one another. On the outside there was always a circle of people looking away from the issue. When I asked who these people were, I was told that they were people who "didn't care." What was missing from the sculpture were the lives of the people who "didn't care" — the activities with which they were already busy (family, work, other issues and projects). The challenge for the organizer is moving social energy — making the group/cause we are working with *the* most important and exciting activity in people's lives.

No matter how busy people are, the amount of time they are willing and able to devote to an activity is elastic. It expands if people are excited and interested and shrinks if they find it boring or irrelevant. This is called "social energy." The conduct of groups and causes can create social energy or shrink it. The following factors can build the social energy of a group:

- The group members have to perceive the group as important, both for themselves and the outside community; working on an issue of great significance will build energy.
- The group allows conflict and open discussion. Such groups have higher participation levels than groups that demand homogeneity (as long as the conflict is not nasty!).
- Tasks are suited to the interests and abilities of participants. Too many groups depend on articulate, formally educated people with a good knowledge of the predominant language. Groups that use domestic skills, artistic skills, manual skills, etc. allow for more diverse participation;
- Groups with a facilitating leadership generally have more participation in the long run than groups with an authoritarian leadership.
- The group is democratic. This nurtures the members and the group will thrive.
- The need for clear rules and avenues for decision-making is even greater in groups that are non-hierarchical in structure, in order to protect individual dignity.

Building a Feeling of "We"

We can judge the cohesion of a group by the number of times people say "you" instead of "we" and by the number of people who keep on talking to their neighbour while the larger meeting is going on. Groups have a social climate: some groups feel nasty, some feel warm. Participants usually express this in terms of who is in the group, saying things like "everyone here is so picky/so uptight/so wonderful/so committed." However, I have seen people who were jerks in one setting be kind and cooperative in another. How we organize our groups will shape the way the people relate to each other.

It is easy to create a feeling of "we" if people come together and identify a common enemy. At the beginning of the long 1978–9 Inco strike, Wives Supporting the Strike spent a great deal of effort creating a float for the Santa Claus parade. On the day of the parade, the diesel truck that was to pull it ran out of gas while it was idling and the float didn't get in the parade. Everyone was very upset, and they all began to blame each other. It was only when they decided that it was an Inco plot to keep them out of the parade that they managed to pull themselves back together as a group. Although this provided a convenient shortcut to solidarity, it would not have been enough to hold the group together for the long haul.

The "enemy" is structural. It is a product of human labour, and we collude in creating it. One of the forms of collusion is giving it more power than it has: for example, if we build strategies organized around our perception of the "enemy" instead of our own collective strength. As it turned out the most effective group process in the Wives Supporting the Strike was around the clothing depots, bean suppers and Christmas parties they held to keep the community together. They were visible achievements; they provided immediate help to those who needed it; they could be organized cooperatively using skills that the members already had.

We all lose when we characterize others as an "enemy." We deny humanity to those whom we oppose; we deny them the possibility of changing. The "we" feeling in a group is more sustainable when it is a product of its common vision and values. Some of these are immediately visible in the stated purposes and goals of the group, but there are also unspecified values, and these can create difficulties, especially for new members, unless they are named. They can be dress codes, expectations of time and commitment, political beliefs and so on. We don't all have to agree, as long as it is understood what our differences are.

Cohesion in a group is really a product of the trust people have in one another, and trust is built on honesty and respect. It can only develop through experience, and it is only possible where members of a group feel safe to express opposition or differences. Boredom is often a clue that people are hiding feelings of anger or frustration. Either get differences out in the open or recognize that the group has real limitations in what it can do together. Take time in groups to check in with each other personally.

Dealing with Cliques, Scapegoats and Trouble Makers

There is no reason to assume that a group should include everyone. The group should be clear about who it wants to participate and what the terms of membership are: those who agree with the goals of ABC; those who are invited to join; anyone at all?

Most groups have an invisible organization as well as a visible one. The invisible organization can be made up of friendships, people who see each other frequently at work or other places, people who share social class, race, gender, skills and so on. The larger the organization the more likely it is to develop these sub-groupings. If the visible structure of the organization does not recognize and correspond to the invisible structures, then there is going to be serious trouble. If a group pretends it has no leaders, or its real leaders do not correspond to the elected ones, then it cannot hold them accountable for their behaviour. Further, it is hard on the un-named leaders, because they are afraid to exercise their leadership with any consistency. Everyone feels insecure.

It is normal for some people to like each other more and for some people to not get along. Although people don't always have to be nice to each other, they do have to respect other members' feelings. In fact, being nice to each other all the time eventually makes a group feel dishonest. People need to feel safe to express their true feelings and worries in a group. Take time to talk personally, to check in with each other.

As an organizer I may really dislike some members of the group and it affects my ability to work with them. If I am serious about helping the group succeed, I need to have someone else in the group work with those people. My personal likes and dislikes are not as important as the work.

Sometimes groups that are stymied in their progress try to avoid their own responsibility by picking on one member (often the staff person). In social change organizations, the scapegoat will usually quit when this happens. Occasionally, the blame is warranted and their quitting is a healthy solution. However, in situations where a series of people have quit an organization, it is useful to ask ourselves if we create scapegoats for our own failings and then drive them out. I have been part of groups where the leadership consistently forced the resignation of any person who stood up to them. We were only able to change the pattern by setting up a discussion that included all the people who had been forced to resign. Perhaps, also, such a group would benefit from training in group dynamics, listening skills or other interpersonal development.

There are some people who are so dysfunctional in groups that people begin to think they are police or company agents. In fact, it doesn't matter if they are or not, the effect is the same. If there is someone in a group that is consistently bullying, dogmatic, disruptive and/or damaging to group process, then that person should be asked to leave. It does no one any good to keep pretending. It might work to send a few people from the group to talk privately with the person about their behaviour. If the person is a paid staff, make sure that issues of "wrongful dismissal" are considered and that the group has documented the problems and followed due process.

In social change groups, there is often a "lone ranger" — someone who has been carrying the issue by themselves, often for decades, and does not really want anyone else to take on leadership. This person may have developed all sorts of passive-aggressive techniques for discouraging others from getting involved. Examples include forgetting to let people know about meetings or setting them at inappropriate times; downloading overly technical information that intimidates others; expecting too much from group members. Although the group may be grateful for the leader's dedication, they have to find ways to dilute their power. If this can't be done subtly, then the group (together) will need to confront them, perhaps with the assistance of a mediator.

Understanding Group Growth and Change

It is the norm of organizations to shift and change. They go through different stages, and like our children, what they become when they grow up is often very different from what we had anticipated. The groups we want to build are very different from the institutions that enshrine power-over. In most cases we do not have access to large and consistent sources of income, so we cannot maintain staff. Members are changed by the group and by the other things that happen in their lives. Some of the people go on to organize around other issues and with other people. Some move away. Some of them just return to their old lives. Some become burned out.

Even when we do establish permanent organizations, they look different from the original activist bunch and different from the dreams we had. We may mobilize people around an issue, or run an election campaign, or win a strike, with enormous outputs of personal energy and commitment, but setting up a long-term organization is a different matter. We look for funding, but it is usually for service-oriented rather then advocacy work. Eric Shragge argues that social change groups should not institutionalize for this reason.[1]

Low-income teenagers in downtown Kingston fought for and ran no less than three youth drop-in centres in the late 1960s. The authorities would close them down on some pretext or another, and the kids would mobilize and get another one. Eventually, the young people who were part of this struggle grew up. The men who were part of the centres originally did not stay involved in social change, but the girls went on to organize a women's centre, a transition house and a locally owned clothing operation.

In fact, this process of group growth and change is a result of the dance between the forces for liberation and hope and the systems of domination and control. We push for change; they shift enough to accommodate some of our demands, but they still retain control. We push for an end to violence against women in their homes; they offer us transition houses and minimum wages to staff them. We push for neighbourhood control over health care; they give us a walk-in clinic. We push for better working conditions; they give us stress workshops.

The product of our groups should be to sustain the effort to effect shifts in power, to build a culture of resistance, to strengthen community leaders and to redistribute wealth, not to build institutions for their own sake. The groups we build and the activities we take on are part of the larger global justice movement and the issue-centred movements (like food sovereignty) that compose it. We do not have to do everything. We need to trust others to do what needs to be done.

Different Kinds of Groups for Different Purposes

Recognizing the kind of group we need is important. What distinguishes groups from one another is the amount of time and energy members are willing to commit to the group, their size, whether their focus is single-issue or multi-issue, whether members are individuals or organizational representatives, and duration.

Small Groups of People with Little Time or Energy Commitment around Specific Issues

In these groups, often job-related, members meet once a month to share information, or strategize about an activity, a political concern or something. An example might be a coordinating committee against wife assault. Most participants are not willing to put a lot of time into the work of the group, although a few often expect a great deal from it. There are often serious differences in values and methods within the group. To function effectively, the group should be very clear about its goals and expectations from the membership.

Small Groups of Highly Committed People

These passionate groups usually self-select members around an issue or project. They depend on the personality and skills of the members, and emotions play a large role in their effectiveness. It is important for the members of the group to be clear with one another about expectations and goals and to realize that the group will change as time goes on. The group is often relatively short-lived, although it may be very effective.

Collectives of Eight to Fifteen People

A group of this size offers the greatest possibility for truly sharing decision-making and building commitment. Depending on the amount of time and energy people are willing to commit to the group, it can accomplish a great deal. Consensus is the most effective form of decision-making in a group of this size. Some collectives take on intense projects: theatre, civil disobedience and so on. Many collectives have to rely on a mixture of paid staff and volunteers to carry out their services, and often have a plan for wage parity. If they seek funding from government or donors, they will either have to find a sponsoring organization or set up a board of directors that does not include voting staff members. Some collectives later incorporate themselves as worker cooperatives.

As collectives often form out of a friendship between the participants, it is really important to agree — from the beginning — on a process for adding new members and also for getting rid of members who may, over time, become dysfunctional in the group. People can burn out, get sick, start drinking too much or just move away from the collective's vision. It will be difficult to remove someone after they have been in the group for a long time, especially if they are on a salary. One dysfunctional member can make working in the collective so unpleasant that it is destroyed.

Campaign Mobilizations

This kind of group forms around a single issue — to protest a rent increase, or to stop a mine or support a strike. Large numbers of people from differing backgrounds come together for a short-term, powerful action or series of actions.

These groups are usually characterized by a strong leadership that is very committed to the issue. Organizing can provide opportunities for education of many people on the issue and related issues, for leadership development and for the building of networks outside the community. The leadership often feels it cannot take the time to do this work with the membership. As a result, although people stay on board for the duration of the struggle, they may then leave, feeling used and burned out.

Many mass mobilizations use a non-hierarchical model developed by the Clamshell Alliance in the United States during the 1980s. They developed a structure with "affinity groups" to sustain non-violent civil disobedience around a single issue. This method was used very effectively in The Battle of Seattle.

The Clam developed the following principles for structure:

- New members who want to join the Clam are required to take an intensive training in non-violent action and the issues. The ten to fifteen people who take the training together form an "affinity group" in a local area and elect a "spoke" to sit on the coordinating committee.
- A committee is established to coordinate the decisions of local groups, not to make them.
- All action is to be non-violent, direct action.
- All action is to have the same specific focus.
- Each local group maintains its own existence.
- The local group most directly affected has veto rights on any action. If other groups don't agree they just don't participate in the action.
- Affinity groups are the vehicle of decision-making and training.
- Spokes bring ideas, decisions and proposals to a larger group of spokes, but all decisions are made in affinity groups.

This method builds security, community, ownership of the action, good training and allows decisions on the spot. The original group of people who started the Clamshell Alliance took responsibility for setting up the training workshops and recruiting membership and later became accountable to the coordinating committee. Subsequently, affinity groups have been adapted for many large mobilizations, including environmental blockades like Clayquot Sound and anti-globalization protests. Chris Hurl provides a useful analysis of the key strengths and weaknesses of this model:

> Of course, this organizational model did not always work.... Significant divisions developed as these organizations expanded. In some cases, formal consensus could not be achieved and decision-making moved to a voting model based on a 2/3 or 3/4 majority. The organization of action outside the consensus process became problematic. For instance, the Clamshell Alliance crumbled under criticisms of an informal leadership who were unilaterally making decisions outside of the consensus process. Further, the maintenance of a nonviolent orthodoxy did not curtail the divergence of strategic and tactical orientations. While some activists sought to halt the construction of nuclear power plants through direct action, others feared that this would alienate the rural communities and instead tried to organize demonstrations.
>
> The translation of this model by the Direct Action Network to the organization of direct action in Seattle proved to be quite success-ful. It enabled the coordination of decentralized groups functioning relatively autonomously to effectively shut down the WTO's first day of meetings. Groups were organized and networked together on a series of levels, building from affinity groups to affiliated clusters which were then distributed as wedges of a pie encircling the con-ference centre. Decisions were made in a direct, decentralized and timely fashion and were effectively communicated to other groups enabling the adaptation of action to changing circumstances. With the success of Seattle, this model was reinvigorated and widely ap-plied to actions all over the world.
>
> However, the translation of this organizational model to large scale urban protests was not without its problems. The lack of a clear correspondence between organizations and the space of action made the maintenance of broad parameters of action untenable. There was no way to ensure that these parameters could be maintained. The Seattle actions brought together a number of disparate groups in a temporary convergence which could no longer be defined organizationally, but led to the coexistence of multiple forms of organization in a shared space and time. With the coexistence of multiple communities in this extensive space, a nonviolent discipline could not be maintained.[2]

Multi-Issue Organizations

Residents' associations and community centres, like Sudbury Better Beginnings Better Futures, are multi-issue organizations. They require the negotiation of different interests and concerns in the group in order to build a power base to achieve an agreed-upon end. It is important to be very clear about the goals of the organization. These groups are hard to hold together, especially if they are not incorporated. There is a tendency for everyone to be running off in a different direction. The work of multi-issue organizations can be facilitated by the use of autonomous task groups for different activities.

Meetings can easily become nightmares. They need to be carefully structured so that they provide opportunity for lots of participation from the membership. Otherwise, people will feel that their issues are not being looked after, and nasty power struggles can ensue. Although the group needs to work from a consensus about its purpose, decision-making structure and goals, it cannot operate by consensus. The group needs room for people to disagree with one another without having to be endlessly in meetings trying to come to consensus. It needs at least one activity in which all members participate. It needs lots of opportunities for leadership development and education.

Sometimes it is useful for special interests within the organization to form "caucuses" — groupings of people who share a commitment to the organization but want to see it be more responsive to their needs. Often the caucuses are based on gender, race or class differences within the organization. Sometimes there is an informal caucus of smokers who meet outside the hall. Caucuses should be democratically constituted.

As multi-issue organizations often have a paid staff, they can run into problems with the provincial or national offices or with funders trying to dictate their issues and structure. Nevertheless, when they do succeed in truly representing grassroots interests, or in uniting diverse interests in a common cause, they can present a real threat to the status quo.

Coalitions

Coalitions are composed of a number of groups and organizations that agree formally to work together around a common issue. Although working this out can be very time consuming, they need to be very clear on the purpose and statement of the coalition.

Representatives to the coalition have to deal with the internal politics of their own organizations on the issue, and this can be difficult, especially if the coalition has to move quickly. Representatives need to be sure they can bring their organization along with the coalition. The coalition might find that the target of its pressure calls its bluff, and they will need to mobilize support from all the member groups. This is facilitated if the coalition has a very clear process for decision-making.

The purpose of coalitions is not to build total unity; neither should they drown the member organizations over a few differences. The idea is to unite on what you can agree on. Member groups should be free to continue to wage their own activities and campaigns.

When MiningWatch Canada was established, although the members were organizations, it was decided to have board members sit as individuals, precisely to avoid organizational gridlock. Although this facilitated decision-making, it also led to situations where the member groups sometimes broke ranks to side with the mining industry. The executive director of one of MiningWatch's founding organizations went to work for the mining industry lobby.

Because of the diversity of interests, personal networks can create jealousies and power struggles within a coalition. Broad-based coalitions that include organizations of different races, genders and classes have to be careful not to tokenize participants.

Networks

The internet has enabled the creation of broad networks of people and organizations who want to share information, analyses and strategies with one another. Usually there is a network administrator, but anyone in the network can contribute. They are profoundly democratic and egalitarian. The World Social Forums, the global justice demonstrations, the peace movement and many of the actions in solidarity with community struggles are made possible with computer networking.

Although they may be a component of a strategy for change, networks do not measure their success in terms of concrete changes in the power structure, but in their size and in their ability to affect consciousness and to give voice to a particular point of view or vision.

Decisions have to be made early on about who can join a network or listserve. Is it open or closed? What are the strategic implications? Who will moderate the listserve?

One of the most successful networks I know is the Western Mining Action Network (WMAN), which is made up of grassroots groups and a few national and regional organizations from the United States and Canada. Started in the mid-1990s, the WMAN raises money for a half-time staff person and a meeting of members every two years in different regions, where workshops and plenary sessions provide educational opportunities for mining activists and community leaders to share strategies, research and resources with each other. It has an excellent website[3] and listserve, which continue the work of the conference. Through a partnership with the Indigenous Environmental

Network, Indigenous WMAN participants now make up about 50 percent of the organization. It is governed by a steering committee of twenty or so people elected by regional, Indigenous and youth caucuses. As the WMAN is not incorporated, one of its member groups acts as a fiscal agent. Although it does not campaign itself, all members must subscribe to its environmental justice principles and objectives.

Empowering Organizations

During my 1998 tour of eleven major cities in Canada while working with the Urban Issues Program of the Samuel and Saidye Bronfman Family Foundation, I visited more than 250 groups and activists who were involved in urban community development work. Urban Issues was probably the most innovative funding program in Canada at that time. Its program resulted from a meeting of architects, academics and activists in the late 1980s, where they drafted the North Hatley statement. In summary, the statement advocated that economic decisions must be integrated with ecological, cultural and social concerns and values, and that "people are empowered when they create a political system, where through actions, elections and referenda they exercise real community and democratic control in order to effect the changes they desire." The program believed that the answer lay in "the formation of citizen associations which encourage people to have an impact on their environment, economics, politics and culture"[4]

The tour was an opportunity for me to learn from cutting edge urban social activists across the country. Since the Urban Issues Program only funded projects to a maximum of $30,000 a year for three years, I was charged with looking at how any of the projects might actually contribute to building organizations for community control. The projects were diverse, ranging from community arts, to the re-opening of a buried creek-bed, to community economic development programs and housing. However, the projects' long-term effectiveness in contributing to social change depended on how they related to other organizations in the community.

The most important factor in the projects' success was their choice of a sponsoring organization. Any project needing funding will be asked by potential donors to identify a sponsor. Usually, the "choice" is about taking whatever we can get among organizations that have charitable status and sufficient administrative capacity. Some sponsors only provide a name. Others, through their base and their work, create a dynamic relationship with the project that is empowering to the community. Examples of organizations that can be effective sponsors include family support centres, housing cooperatives and environmental organizations.

The *empowering organizations* share most of the following characteristics:

- *People from the community are in charge* ("community" being defined as either a neighbourhood or a minority racial connection in common). Sometimes, the organization might consist of a constellation of different organizations and groups, but they have some means of working and making decisions together, or are working towards this. The "organization" may not have a large membership base, but it has the support and respect of its community and undertakes programs which involve the community as equals. The formal leadership of the organization is similar to the actual leadership.
- *The leadership has the ability and will to build the power of the community to determine its future.* They have an understanding of the relationship of the organization to the larger picture (environmentally, economically, politically, culturally), are thirsty for knowledge and know how to take learnings back to the community. They are holistic in their approach.
- *The organization has programs that seek out and encourage participants who are committed, imaginative, skilled and willing to take risks for one another and their community.* It builds the capacity of the community to act. It works to research and develop the information and analysis the community needs in forms that local people can understand and use
- *The organization wants to work with others to continue to develop critical thinking and understanding, to learn from and challenge one another, to build movement, to plan strategies.* It participates in strategy to put what it has been learning forward to decision-makers, to influence policy and to help "the new paradigm" to emerge.

The following are stumbling blocks to creating and maintaining empowering organizations:

- *The need for charitable status in order to receive funds from donors and foundations is a huge problem for organizations that want to do lobbying and political work as well as provide services.* Empowering organizations often have to incorporate more than one body to do this. For example, MiningWatch set up the Canary Research Institute on Mining, Environment and Health. Sudbury Better Beginnings Association also has the Sudbury Better Beginnings Educational Fund. This creates an extra administrative burden for the organization but may be the only option. We need to find a lawyer that specializes in non-profit law to do this; lawyers without this specific knowledge may think they know what they are doing but probably don't. Tides Canada has set up the Sage Foundation to provide a sponsor for activist projects which need foundation support but do not have charitable status. Sage puts 90 percent of its grants into unquestionable charities like hospitals and educational institutions so that the remaining 10 percent can support political work.

- *Board structures are a problem.* Workers are over-worked and often alienated from the board, and executive directors generally hold too much power and responsibility, as they are often solely responsible to the board for staff performance. This is a recipe for burn-out. Allowing all staff to attend board meetings and organizing the staff as a collective that nominates its executive director to the board can go a long way to alleviating this situation.
- *Reporting requirements from funders make it difficult for neighbourhood people to be involved in the boards.* They find it confusing and boring, and the number of picayune issues that need to be discussed by the board use up the meeting time. The much-vaunted "Carver" model does not help either. Neighbourhood folk and local activists find it almost impossible to discuss policy in the abstract: they want to get into the details and concrete examples. Empowering organizations have usually found creative ways to involve the neighbourhood in discussing issues in a concrete manner and to make accounting interesting and transparent.
- *We need community organizers to organize.* Someone needs to be out there meeting people face-to-face on a regular basis, building relationships and bringing people together when they have issues in common. Facebook may help maintain relationships but it does not create them. These people may not be called organizers; they may have titles like family support worker or para-legal, but their job description has to include organizing. The organizers need a flexible mandate. They need enthusiasm and creativity.
- *Many organizations are forced into service delivery models that "clientize" the community.* McKnight says a client is "one who is controlled." People are divided into helpers and helpees. This profoundly disempowering distinction is reproduced in the style, structure and practice of the organizations. Those who would become agents in changing their reality instead become passive recipients of a service. When this is compounded by similar treatment from welfare, landlords, food banks and every service with which the person interacts, the result is devastating. It takes real consciousness and effort to avoid this organizational culture and create a different one.

Notes

1. Eric Shragge, *Activism and Social Change* (Peterborough, ON: Broadview Press, 2003). Good examples and analysis of community development and its limitations.
2. Chris Hurl, "Anti-Globalization and Diversity of Tactics" *Upping the Anti* 1, April 22, 2005 <http://uppingtheanti.org/journal/article/01-anti-globalization-and-diversity-of-tactics>.
3. Western Mining Action Network <http://www.wman-info.org/>.
4. Urban Issues Program archives <sfu.ca/humanities-institute/archive/bronfman.htm>.

7

Making Meetings Work

Meetings are the occasions for democratic process to happen. They are the place where members of a group meet each other face to face to learn, make decisions and reflect. In these meetings we expect to come to agreement. Another kind of meeting takes place when we negotiate, get information or confront structures from whom we want to take power. In these we want to clarify areas of disagreement and make a show of our strength and unity. Meetings can be composed of any number of people. Their size varies with their purpose and, of course, with how many people we can attract. Meetings should be interesting and fun. They are all about creating and maintaining enthusiasm. This discussion of meetings is divided into two parts: meetings where one of the objectives is to build unity and meetings where the objective is to show strength.

Meetings to Build Unity

Success in a meeting can mean different things to different people. For community organizers who are interested in a movement for social change, one yardstick should be that people at the meeting felt good enough about it to come to another. Other measures would be lots of participation from members and accomplishing the task of the meeting (even if the task were to decide on a task).

There are some fairly simple guidelines for interesting and democratic meetings. If the rules are followed, the meeting should go well.

Consensus decision-making is okay when everyone agrees on the basic principles or when the group is small. Where the group is task-oriented and there is not agreement on basic principle, it is death. The discussion can drag on forever. It can also encourage an elite leadership who manipulate the minority, making real debate difficult. Where time is limited and there is an entrenched opposition, it may be necessary to hold a vote on the issue.

To enable maximum participation, break the large group in to small table groups of four or five people and/or buzz groups of two or three to discuss their ideas about matters up for discussion in the plenary. This process provides some safety for shy people who want to express their opinion and ensures that important matters have been thoroughly considered by everyone in the room. It builds relationships among the participants and makes it harder for the most articulate people to dominate the discussion. Feedback from the groups can be informal, asking if anyone has something they want to share with the larger group; formal feedback may become tedious if it is a large meeting.

Setting up task groups or committees to report back to the larger group can move a big agenda along quickly. These groups should be as autonomous as possible, so that everyone has a share in decision-making. Where non-violent, direct action or other high-risk activities are planned, people on the firing line need to control the decisions that affect them.

Taking time to laugh and play together is always worth it, as is a break to go for a walk, play a cooperative game or tell some jokes. Even in a tense meeting this can quickly change the atmosphere. One of the Aboriginal co-chairs of MiningWatch Canada was particularly adept at diffusing tension with a raunchy joke. Silence can be an important part of decision-making, as can well-timed breaks, which give people time to caucus together informally.

Always take time to celebrate our victories and each other. We all need recognition and lots of it. People need time to report in on their achievements.

The Facilitator

Any meeting with more than five people needs a facilitator/chair: someone who will be responsible for process, making sure that no one dominates and everyone gets a chance to participate. The facilitator can be chosen by the group at a previous meeting or as the first item on an agenda. If it is our first meeting together, we should ask someone to facilitate the meeting.

The facilitator/chair should not actively contribute to discussion, especially if the matters are contentious. They are to act as a referee for the conversation to keep it on track and make sure everyone gets a chance to express their opinion. Occasionally, when a meeting is full of conflict, the facilitator may have to make judgement calls about what has been said, who has talked too much and when people want to decide something. If a facilitator takes flak for this, they can turn it back to the participants, asking for a straw vote for or against the decision.

Rotating the chair is not always a good idea: this is a skilled trade. We should train facilitators and secretaries, etc. so that more people can do these tasks, but not at the expense of messing up a difficult meeting. The spokesperson and the chair of a meeting should never be the same people. Neither should the person with the most information chair a meeting.

Outside facilitators can be asked in to help move a group along. Make sure, however, that the group has approved this process before the facilitator takes the chair, and be careful that the facilitator is culturally appropriate to the group. I have seen an outside facilitator, whose experience was with the male-dominated conservation movement, completely wreck a meeting where women and Indigenous people were the key participants. The meeting was only saved when we kicked him out and one of the Aboriginal women took over the facilitation.

Large Meetings

The following ideas can help ensure that everyone gets to participate in a large meeting:

Open space conferencing provides a simple way for people to self-organize around issues of concern to them. Sitting in a large circle, participants learn how they are going to create their own conference. Anyone who wants to initiate a discussion or activity writes it in big letters on a large sheet of paper and announces it to the group. They choose a meeting time and place from a grid of post-it notes provided by organizers, and then tape their session announcement up on a scheduling wall. When everyone has announced their initial offerings, the conference begins. No one is in control. The practice has a few simple principles like:

1. Whoever comes are the right people.
2. Whatever happens is the only thing that could have.
3. Whenever it starts is the right time.
4. When it's over it's over.[1]

The World Café allows a large group to have the intimacy and engagement of small group dialogue without losing the broader understandings and group-feeling of plenary sessions. It requires space for groups of four to six people to sit in circles. After thirty to forty-five minutes of conversation a bell tells tablemates to choose one of their number to stay behind while the others move to new tables to share what emerged from their earlier discussions. The bell continues to move participants to new tables at regular intervals, but ultimately they return to their original tables to share what they learned.[2]

Rules for Successful Meetings

Before the Meeting
- Be sure about the meeting's purpose before starting, and then confirm with the whole group that they are agreed on the purpose.

- Meetings have to be at convenient times and places. Only people with university educations are comfortable meeting in universities, and middle-class people may be uncomfortable in a drop-in centre. We need to choose the meeting place and time that will attract the kind of people we want to have in the group.
- Think about whether participants can get to the meeting. What about obstructive husbands, wives, parents, bosses? What about childcare/eldercare arrangements? Farm-sitting? Availability of transport? If this is the first meeting for some people, it might be a good idea to arrange for someone to bring them. It can be pretty scary going to our first meeting.
- Having food at the meeting changes the atmosphere and creates unity. What about potluck dinners, cooking together or taking turns providing coffee?
- Arrange chairs and tables (if there are any) to maximize participation. Sitting people in a circle equalizes power in a group. If the circle gets too big, however, and we cannot hear each other speak, then it is oppressive. Microphones make it easier for people to hear, but they restrict participation. For large groups, use concentric semi-circles with a facilitator or "table groups" set up so everyone can see the facilitator easily.
- Make sure to have all the equipment needed for the meeting: films, flipcharts, markers, projectors, etc.; make up a list ahead of time and check it off.

The Conduct of the Meeting
- Meetings should not be too long, and the beginning and ending time should be adhered to unless the group decides differently.
- Meetings should have a sense of creative play, of learning and of purpose. People get bored if they can't participate or if they are holding in their anger and frustration. We all have lives that are too busy to waste time in irrelevant or boring meetings.
- At the beginning of a meeting, it is often a good idea to have a check-in, where people talk a little bit about how they are feeling and what baggage they are bringing to the meeting. In a larger group this can be done in small groups, using one of the community building exercises. We cannot assume everyone knows each other.
- The agenda should be agreed upon by the people there. If there is too much to cover in one session, make sure that people know when their pet issue will be dealt with. If there are strong divisions in the group, make sure all sides are comfortable with the agenda.
- Make sure that the results of the meeting are recorded, so that everyone can see what happened. This job can be rotated as long as the records are kept in a convenient place. In asking for volunteers for this, remem-

ber that many people are illiterate or don't know how to take minutes. The role of secretary is a powerful one, and it is important to make sure participants get an early opportunity to review the minutes and make corrections.

- It is important to keep conflict from being cruel or mean. People are too busy to stay if every meeting is unpleasant. If people are in serious conflict with one another, they can be asked to leave the meeting and come back with a compromise position that they can both agree on.

Meetings to Show Strength

These meetings are set up by others — usually those identified with the power structures, sometimes when we are actually negotiating with representatives of a power structure. There are a few basic rules.

The first rule is to be clear about what the group wants from the meeting. Is it just to obtain information? Or do we expect to get a decision? Or do we just want to show the structure our strength? Are we sure that what we ask from the people we are meeting with is within their power to give? If we are only meeting with them to test their response, be clear about that too.

We should *never* argue among ourselves in the opposition's presence, unless our purpose is to show them how democratically our group operates. If we need to discuss something with each other, we should leave the meeting to talk, or ask them to leave while we talk, or save our disagreement for later.

We should where possible decide on spokespeople before the meeting and support them. We can be sure that the efforts of the other side will be directed at dividing us. We can't allow our spokespeople to leave the group to talk with the other side. If they have something to discuss it should be done in front of the whole group. In some situations, like a government-sponsored meeting on a toxic waste site, we may want all our members to speak at the meeting. That's okay as long as we understand beforehand why we are doing it and what people will say.

It is important to debrief as soon as possible with the whole group after the meeting to evaluate what we achieved and how people felt about it.

Notes

1. For more information, see <http://www.openspaceworld.com/users_guide.htm> or Harrison Owen, *Open Space Technology: A User's Guide* (San Francisco: Berrett-Koehler, 1997).
2. See <http://www.co-intelligence.org/P-worldcafe2.html>.

8

Research

Elizabeth May writes: "The base (for your organizing) must be solid. Your base is research. You must have your facts straight. Find out everything you can about the issue."[1]

In our work, we often need scientific and technical information that is difficult for many people to understand or access. Sometimes this research exists, and other times it doesn't. Invariably it will be in a language and form that most of us don't understand. Often we need someone to translate complex technical language into something we can understand and discuss. Most experts have a lot of trouble doing this and can be defensive when they are repeatedly asked to explain something.

The best kind of research for community groups is something called "participatory research": investigations that work from people's own experience and help the community or group figure out what actions they need and can take to change the situation. When people collectively analyze and build their knowledge about their lives, they are empowering themselves. We can probably find people in a nearby university to help us learn how to research issues for ourselves. The kind of research that involves the community members in examining their own reality goes by different names: participatory research, participatory rural appraisal, participatory action research, community-based research and so on. This research puts as much or more emphasis on the process as on the results. It is closely allied with popular education.

We can borrow some of the techniques that participatory researchers and popular educators have developed, such as the web, force-field analysis, forum theatre, and historical mapping.[2] If we have decided to use a survey of the community to get information, it helps to remember that different kinds of surveys produce different results. If the group wants to get people in the community involved, it is counter-productive to treat the survey subjects like statistics. After the study, we will want to talk them about other issues and matters. On the other hand, if the group is just interested in verifiable data, it will have to do an anonymous, random-sample, highly structured survey. Most academic researchers will have to deal with codes of ethics, confidentiality requirements and so on. Although these give credibility to aggregated survey results, they will make it impossible to use the survey as a door-to-door organizing tool. We need to be clear about why we are doing it before we decide on a method.

Where can we get the information we need about our community? Our group can go together to get information we need from experts and share it. This is much more empowering than asking an expert to do it for us. The internet is of course a great source, but we need to be careful about the reliability of the information. Some of it is simply untrue. A lot of information is available at public libraries, and the librarians are often very willing to help. Some of the information can be found in the city files or the economic development office. It is our right as a citizen to know this information, so make it a political point to ask for it.

The following are some suggestions for getting the basic research community activists often need:

- *Land ownership:* These can be researched at registry office files. It costs money and a small amount of expertise. Try to find a lawyer or law clerk who will help decipher the records. A lot of land is held by corporations. The owners of the corporations are usually required to register with the Companies Branch of the provincial government, and this information can be requested.
- *Government policies and practices:* Regulations and laws are all public information and are usually available from the internet. They can also be found in libraries and from government departments, although we may need to file an Access to Information request to get it. We should feel free to ask public servants or members of Parliament for help. That's their job.
- *Historical information:* This is available from the internet, libraries, interviews, newspaper files, company archives and so on. We can also undertake a participatory activity in the community to find out what people know.
- *Information on corporate structures, behaviour, policies:* There are a number of NGOs that specialize in corporate research in particular areas. All public corporations (those with shares) have to register with the Securities Commission and file a number of documents annually. These are available on the internet at <sedar.com>. Some corporations have archives that we can access by pretending we are a student researcher. Some corporate information is available to shareholders, and it is worthwhile buying a share to get access to the information. Sometimes we need a "mole": someone who will leak information to us from inside the structure. Financial papers carry a surprising amount of information.

We can research these at our local library or on the internet. There are a number of public advocacy organizations that have extensive files on corporations and are willing to help us do the research.

- *Information on toxics, pollution, etc.:* A number of organizations specialize in researching these areas and making the information available to the public. Check out <pollutionwatch.ca>, a website run by Environment Canada that will tell us the toxins in our region by postal code. Environmental Defence Canada has a Toxic Nation campaign. The Sierra Club of Canada undertakes a great deal of work on toxics. In the United States, the most effective organization is the Centre for Health, Environment and Justice, which was founded by Lois Gibbs. A great deal can be found on the internet. Unfortunately, there are also corporate-sponsored groups with websites that exist to hide the truth from the public. Always get information from more than one source where possible.
- *Peoples' history/social activism:* Doing a research project to record the history of people's struggles in our own area is a valuable and interesting activity. There are also a large number of theses and books written by university researchers on social change that never get out of the library.
- *Community information:* Knowing about a particular landlord or a road development or an expropriation case may be valuable in planning strategy. This information is collected by asking lots of questions of the people most affected and by demanding information from public officials and businesspeople.

Exercise: Understanding Our Own Community

The following exercise is an example of a participatory research approach to understanding the community. It can be used at any time in a group's life, either to test the relevance of what we are doing at the present time or to make plans for the future. It reveals information about the community we live in so that the flow of money, the kinds of work people do, the power relationships and the possibilities for change are visible to everyone in the group. Often members of the community themselves hold more information collectively than they think. Participants would be local people.

The exercise takes about two or three hours to do. Begin with a large blackboard and chalk or magic markers and a huge sheet of newsprint. Then ask questions similar to the following and "diagram" the participants' answers accordingly:

- What are the major roads?
- What are important buildings? Where are they? (Make sure they tell you about both public and private buildings)

- Where do people congregate?
- Where do people work? What do they do in a day? (If they are unemployed, find out what they do.) How many people work at each kind of work (both paid and unpaid). You can use percentages and just write them down the side. What about men's and women's work? Make sure to include eldercare, childcare, fishing, hunting, gathering, bootlegging, prostitution and drug trafficking as work. Who owns/runs the workplaces? Do they live in the area?
- What are the conditions of work in the major employers? Are there unions?
- Where do people live? Where are the most people? What are their racial differences? Do they eat at home? Where else? Who owns the housing? Where do the owners live? What is the quality of the housing? Who holds the mortgages? Is there land speculation going on? How much of the money in housing stays in the community?
- Where do the people get food? How many people have gardens? Hunt? Forage? Trap? (Ask this even in cities.) Do they buy food in the community? If not, who owns the major stores? Where do the profits go?
- Where do the people get clothing? Do they make their own? If not, where does the clothing come from?
- Where do they get the energy supplies they need? Is any of it renewable?
- What do they do with their sewage? With their garbage?
- What do the people do for entertainment? Who owns the places of entertainment? Include sports in this question and look at the purchase of equipment.
- What about schools? Are the teachers from the community? Do they live in the community? How do the parents, the kids relate to the school? What are the problems? Who makes the money from the purchase of school materials and construction? Does the curriculum have anything to do with the kids' real lives?
- What do the young people do when they are not in school? Where do they hang out? Do they need more activities? What?
- Where are the religious institutions? Which religions are represented? How many active members do they have? Is there conflict between them? Over what issues? How much influence do they have? How would you describe the religious/cultural life of the community?
- What money comes into the community? Do some people have more money than others? How can we tell? What are the class differences in the community? What do the rich do that the poor don't do and vice-versa. Where do people save their money?
- What are the main sources of information in the community? Does the

community control any of these (include gossip)? Who are the community opinion leaders? Who do people trust for advice and information (emphasize informal leadership)? Who do they trust the least?

- Are there community organizations at the grassroots level? What are they? How much support do they have? Who are their leaders? What is our relationship to them? (Don't forget that there may be distinct ethnic and gender divisions here).

Research is something that should involve as many members of the group as possible, and it should be disseminated to everyone. Knowledge is power, and knowledge about the organizing context will shape strategy and tactics. Find ways to share information creatively with other members of the group. For example, if the problem we decide to take on is welfare cutbacks, we can get information from many sources. First we can do a survey of recipients themselves — looking at effects of the cuts, their budgets, how much coping will exhaust them, what organizations do they know that will fight it with them. We can get information from the internet about government statistics and surveys. We can get information from legal clinics and poor people's organizations. We can get it from the national churches and other national organizations like the Canadian Centre for Policy Alternatives. And we can get it from schools of social work and other sociologists. We can also read the financial pages of the paper to see what government is spending its money on instead.

For another example, if the problem we decide to tackle is toxic wastes in our neighbourhood, we can interview our neighbours to see what effect it is having on them and how they feel about it and if they would like to organize. We can talk to the municipal government and the department of public health. We can get information on toxic wastes from organizations like Pollution Probe, Environmental Defence Canada, the Sierra Club, Greenpeace, the Clearing House for Toxic Waste and the Canadian Environmental Law Association. There are a lot of documented stories on the internet and in books and films of citizens' groups that have taken on the toxic waste issue, and we can see how they fought back. Libraries and government offices and United Nations publications all deal with these issues, as do academics in many parts of Canada. Again reports are often on the internet.

In both these examples, we can see that there is a range of ways to get information. The trick is to make this information accessible to different classes and groups of people and to put it all together. Use mapping, drawings and models (like developers use) to work it out and make it visible.

Notes

1. Elizabeth May, *How to Save the World in Your Spare Time* (Toronto: Key Porter, 2006) p. 44.
2. These methods are found in Deborah Barndt, *Naming the Moment* (Toronto: Between the Lines, 1989), and in Rick Arnold, Bev Burke and Carl James, *Educating for a Change* (Toronto: Between the Lines, 1991).

Part 4

Reclaiming the Economy, Healing Our Relationship to the Earth

Community members defending childcare and education

9

Managing the Household

The Burwash Prison Farm

In the mid 1980s, a group of us in Sudbury who had been involved in a lengthy battle over jobs and housing with the various levels of government decided to form an organization called the Sudbury Citizens' Movement. Over the period of a year, we developed an idea for an abandoned prison farm thirty minutes drive from the city on the Trans-Canada Highway.

The prison farm had over 26,000 acres of forest and grasslands. It was on a major canoe route and close to Killarney Park — a provincial park of extraordinary beauty. Three thousand acres were cleared land, and in fact the land had once raised enough food to feed the entire prison population of 700 and a small village that was on the site. Fourteen years before, it had been self-sufficient in vegetables, meat and dairy. The year before the provincial government closed it down in a construction boondoggle, they had put $4.5 million into renovations on the sixty-nine houses, thirty-eight-bed single staff quarters, the six shops and three barns. There was also a gymnasium that had never been used, big enough for two basketball courts. The prison building itself was in ruins.

A feasibility study had been done of the site in 1975 by a large consulting firm indicating that a number of business ideas were feasible but would create only about eight to ten jobs each. Our group spent two entire years working out a plan for the site, and proposed that the former Burwash prison farm was an ideal place for a regenerative form of agriculture and an interlocking set of worker cooperatives engaged in farming, forestry, dairy processing, construction and tourism and for the establishment of a group home for kids who were presently in foster care. Our own study indicated that the plan might be self-sufficient within ten years, but that it would require about a $2 million investment from the province in order to bring the housing and so on back up to standard.

We spent two years pressuring the government to take us seriously and building community support. Finally, we had reached a level of community acceptance where the government was forced to acknowledge us, and they responded by hiring a consulting firm, KPMG, to do a feasibility study. The study cost $80,000. They came to many of the same conclusions we had, but they said we were not feasible… because we could only create thirty-five jobs in five years and would not yet be self-sufficient.

There was no way in their calculations to measure the impact of our proposal on the long-term health of the land or the forest. No way for them to measure the long-term benefits for the children that could be there instead of in a city foster home. No way for them to measure the benefits of restoring the housing instead of tearing it down. They could only measure social benefits by the number of people we would have been able to take off the welfare roles. — Socal Ben = ↓ Welfer only

In fact the indices of "success" were such that the government found *Sold off* it more feasible to sell the land to the Department of National Defence for *& destroyd* $65 an acre for a military training camp and to destroy the houses. And because this enormous document from an expert said that our plan was not "feasible," we were unable to convince the press and the public that it was.

Ecological Economics

Just the mention of the word "economics" is often enough to send people fleeing from the room. It appears to be a mysterious form of knowledge that none of us can understand, and we are afraid of looking stupid. As I said in Chapter Two, "economy" comes from two Greek words, meaning "to manage the household." If we managed our households based only on the money that comes in and the money that goes out, we would have a disaster on our hands. We can de-mystify economics by starting with an analysis of the role of money in our daily lives

Reclaiming economics is about rebuilding our physical relationship *Bring* to the earth: clean air, water and soil, decent shelter, nourishing food in *back* adequate supply, warmth, medicines. How do we create these things for *"Household"* everyone equally, with good work and without depleting the world for our *clean up* grandchildren? How do we live and work together? How do we create this *earth* physical environment for millions of people in the midst of a world already poisoned and plundered? Barbara Brandt, in her book *Whole life Economics*, gives us a clue:

> The Economy is not something "out there," understandable only to the experts. You and I create the economy every day, in the course of our daily lives, with our minds and bodies, our hearts and souls, our skills and dreams and values. We create the economy out of the feelings we have about ourselves and our own worth, through our relationships with each other and through our connections with the

natural world. And if we create the economy, this also means we can change it, through the activities of our daily lives, so that it more fully meets our real needs and expresses our deepest values.[1]

There are a number of community problems we can work out for ourselves within the parameters of the existing system. The solutions include cooperatives, self-reliant agriculture, renewable energy sources, community gardens, alternative schools and projects to clean up and contain toxic waste. These activities also build skills that can contribute to creating alternatives to the existing system. The Canadian Social Economy Research Partnerships has compiled a lengthy list of projects and activities to develop the "social economy," available in a website called the Social Economy Hub.[2] Honor the Earth, an Indigenous organization based in Minnesota, has also published an excellent online resource: *Sustainable Tribal Economies: A Guide to Restoring Energy and Food Sovereignty in Native America.*[3]

This understanding of economics is not new. Since the beginning of the industrial revolution, alternatives to capitalism have been explored through cooperatives, utopian communities and worker control of the places of production. There are also national and global movements composed of local efforts to reclaim control over those parts of the economy that are most essential to life: water, food, shelter, climate, waste management and energy.

We resist enterprises like the tar sands, Walmart and corporate agriculture because they further pillage the planet and our relationships. In the last few decades, the global reach of power elites has been reinforced by de-regulation, privatization, trade and investment agreements. Re-claiming economics is not only about creating alternatives; it means supporting political movements to take on the infrastructure that pillages and destroys community sustainability.

Near Williams, Lake British Columbia, the Tsilquot'in people managed to stop an open pit copper-gold mine — the Prosperity Mine — which would have destroyed the entire Fish Creek water system, which has provided rainbow trout and other foods for them for centuries. Only massive organization by the First Nation and its allies over a fourteen-year period finally resulted in a federal decision to turn down the project.[4]

Ecological/Social Accounting

There is a generalized public suspicion that the way we keep accounts and run our financial system does not work. Especially with the financial crash of 2008, many of us clearly see that the economics of the global financial casino have almost nothing to do with the real economy — the production of the goods and services we need and the jobs that provide our livelihoods.

Corporations are "externalizing machines"; they seek to off-load all the costs they can to individuals and the public sector and to disregard completely other costs of services provided by nature — absorbing waste, providing water, energy and land for industrial processes — and the costs of reproducing and maintaining the health of labour. Even before the financial crash, there was a growing movement to enlarge the system of public accounts to keep track of the depletion of natural capital and of the health of the people, the cultures and the social services of our communities.

Ecological (or social or Gaian) accounting measures the real impacts of the activity on the individual, the household, the community and the ecosystem. As one Indigenous man said to me, "When a scaler looks at a large cedar tree he sees $40 a board foot; I see $4000, because I know the value of the tree to the forest, to the atmosphere and to my people, but I also know what the tiny carvings made from every twig of that tree can sell for."

For example, in evaluating a proposed mine, an ecological ledger would include the following:

- *Present uses of the land* surrounding the site and the benefits to the community from them: cultural and spiritual values of the land on the mine site downstream and within the watershed; informal recreation areas and tourism, wildlife and fish habitat and country food supply; trapping and agricultural production, including home gardens, oxygen production from the forest, trails and pathways from one area to another, waste absorption.
- *Costs in terms of* greenhouse effect, accidents, increased stress, changes in driving patterns for users, loss of arable land, air pollution and noise, disruption of community around the mine, injury to wildlife, effect on house prices both near the mine site and in the area from which the workers are drawn, occupational hazards and costs of production, local retention of profits from production, future maintenance; training and manpower, potential contamination of aquifers and groundwater from leakages and spills.
- *The economic viability of the mine.* Chances are it will only be operating for ten to fifteen years maximum. Where will the waste be placed? How will it be managed? What will happen when the mine closes? Can the mess it leaves behind be fixed? What will it cost to close the mine and remediate the mess it leaves behind? How likely is the company to meet its commitments for clean-up years in the future? What price will be paid by future generations?
- *Are the gems or metals produced by the mine socially useful?* Can they come from recycling instead? Could we conserve to avoid mining them? What will be produced with them?

A thriving ecological economics movement is exploring methods to take all these externalized costs and benefits into account. Pioneered by Kenneth Boulding, Hazel Henderson, Herman Daly, Bob Costanza and Marilyn Waring, ecological economics and full-cost accounting have gained real public acceptance. In 1997, Costanza published a paper in *Nature* that set a value on "ecosystem services" — which he calculated at $33 trillion.[5] "Few economists speak of clean air and clean water as 'externalities' as they once did; the essential logic of accounting for costs is slowly spreading."[6] In the past decade, economics students and their professors have been rebelling in France and other EU countries, demanding "post autistic economics."[7]

However, classical economics still rules the world and groups that want recognition for ecological accounting have to fight for it. One of the areas where ecological economics becomes important is in environmental assessment — the government process of looking at environmental effects before it licenses large projects to proceed. In the fall of 2007, after an intense struggle by affected communities and, for the first time in the history of Canadian environmental assessment, ecological economics led to a refusal of the following three different mine projects:

- The Kemess North Mine was found to be "not in the public interest" because benefits to the First Nation clearly did not justify building a mine with a twelve-year life and an environmental footprint that would last for centuries. The mine would have used pristine Amazay Lake as a tailings dump.
- The Whites Point Quarry on Digby Neck in Nova Scotia was turned down because the community was able to prove that the viable plan they had for their region's future would be ruined by the quarry proposal.
- The Lutsel Ku'e Dene in the Northwest Territories were able to stop an advanced exploration project for uranium mine proposed by Ur-Energy on the grounds that it would seriously affect their culture.

Protecting the Commons

The commons refers to resources that are held collectively by all humans. This can include everything from land, minerals, plants and water, to the products of human labour, to the human genetic code itself. The transformation of the commons into private property is fundamental to the accumulation of wealth and power by elites. The corporate paradigm seeks to transform everything into private property — commodities that can be controlled, bought and sold.

David Bollier writes:

> Some are tangible, while others are more abstract, political, and

cultural. The tangible assets of the commons include the vast quantities of oil, minerals, timber, grasslands, and other natural resources on public lands, as well as the broadcast airwaves and such public facilities as parks, stadiums, and civic institutions. The government is the trustee and steward of such resources, but "the people" are the real owners.

The commons also consists of intangible assets that are not as readily identified as belonging to the public. Such commons include the creative works and public knowledge not privatized under copyright law…. Another large realm of intangible assets consists of scientific and academic research, much of which is supported by the public through government funding. The character of these spaces changes dramatically when they are governed as markets rather than as commons….

Yet entrepreneurs and corporations are now developing ingenious ways to turn these natural commons into exploitable property. Several multinational companies are, for example, seeking to transport huge supplies of freshwater in Northern countries to "thirsty" regions in Saudi Arabia, Morocco, and southern California. Biotech companies are trying to gain proprietary control over agricultural seed-lines that have long been regarded as community assets — for example, by seeking patents for a common yellow bean grown widely in Mexico, as well as for basmati rice and neem plants in India. The human genome is a target of property claims and landowners fighting environmental regulations insist that they "own" wildlife and that the regulations amount to an unconstitutional "taking" by government.[8]

In 2003, the people of Chochabamba, Bolivia successfully protected their drinking water from privatization. A Seed Satyagraha in India[9] has been confronting attempts by Monsanto and other companies to control the diversity of the seed supply. Indigenous peoples and environmental groups in Canada resist industrial development in wilderness areas, sacred spaces and water supplies. In British Columbia, the Haida assert governance over Haida Gwaii, and control logging of the ancient forests. Urban groups fight for parks, community gardens, the re-opening of managed streams and rivers and public spaces. Groups fight bio-piracy, and the patenting of the human genome. Open source software continues to work to make knowledge available to all and to subvert plans to privatize internet communication. An excellent website, <onthecommons.org> links these issues together.

Farmers and consumers resist monoculture and the hoarding of farmlands by the corporate elite. An example of an alternative, land trusts are democratic corporations that hold land in the public interest. They can be non-profits or cooperatives. The land cannot be sold for private profit; land is returned to the trust when and if people leave, in return for a refund of their initial investment plus interest. Land trusts can stop land speculation and other types of profiteering and can provide guidelines for land use within their territory. In Canada, many land trusts are also formed in order to accumulate land for housing in city core areas.

Sustainable Community Economic Development

Despite government attempts to control it, community economic development is a vibrant practice of sustainable, community-based, mutual aid alternatives to the current economic system.

> Community economic development starts the process of returning control and ownership of economic decisions to the people most affected by those decisions.... Starting locally means recognizing that there is such a thing as community economics. It means we have to take our personal economic decisions seriously: are we putting money and resources into the local cooking pot to nourish the neighbourhood, or are we sending our best resources elsewhere?... Starting locally, finally, means linking the local community to the world at large.... But a better and more secure future will ultimately rest on the building blocks of strengthened, independent and interdependent communities. The challenge is to think globally, to keep the Big Picture in focus, and to act locally, because at that level every individual can make a real contribution.[10]

These days, Canadian communities are worried about retaining jobs and attracting money. Conventional economic practice seeks to lure investment and industry to a community with a variety of tax and other incentives. These benefits may include anti-union sentiment, low wages, overlooking environmental problems and a pleasant natural environment for visiting executives or tourists. Most communities are trying to chase a major employer and competing with others to offer the most favourable terms. Even if the community is successful, the employer is likely to be there only a few years and will usurp the entire region's economy: the high wages paid by one employer will decimate minimum wage jobs and small businesses in other sectors, and the remaining businesses will shift to meet the needs of the high-wage employer. This has a name, the "intrusive rentier syndrome."[11]

Community economic development (CED) can be a radical departure from this approach. In the hands of social activists, it is about creating self-reliant communities that are less dependent on outside investment. Sustainable community economic development has the following special characteristics:

- It values the informal economy: the work and production that goes on but does not show up in the gross national product: child care, gardening, volunteer work, doing our own repairs, driving each other around, looking after the sick, the aged and the young and so on.
- It is concerned about retaining wealth in a community. It asks "where does the money go" as much as "where does it come from." It favours local ownership and control of business, not trying to get another branch plant or franchise established. It looks at replacing imported products and services with local ones.
- It is as concerned about creating viable communities for our grandchildren as for ourselves. Because they will have to live with environmental effects and social spinoffs, we want to do things correctly now. We pay attention to waste, garbage and sustainability.
- It is about producing socially useful products, like housing and food, not just more consumer junk, harmful products (like military equipment) or hazardous waste dumps.
- It is about development that does not displace the already impoverished residents or depopulate rural communities.
- It is about redistributing the wealth and services in a community so that they may be more equally shared by all.
- It is concerned about the viability of cultural, spiritual and social life.
- It is about creating good work: work that is healthy, satisfying and secure. It is about improving and diversifying the skills of community members.

Need community support as little more crucial

However, even CED enterprises in Canada have to exist within the market economy. That means they must compete with other businesses in order to survive. They are under many of the same pressures as other businesses to pay low wages, to cut back on quality and to ignore environmental concerns. It is thus essential to build strong community support for the sustainable project so that people will be willing to pay a little higher price for quality, ecological soundness and justice.

Practitioners of sustainable CED know that failure rates for small businesses in Canada are high for the first three years and decline over time. About 70 percent of small businesses survive for one full year; half survive for three years. Approximately 25 percent are still operating after nine years. The number of business bankruptcies in Canada fell by 50 percent between 1997 and 2007, to about 6300.[12]

Given high failure rates, we need to ask some hard questions. How are working peoples' wages used to start small businesses or purchase real estate in the town? To what extent are they being used to provide private capital for ventures that just return these hard earned savings to the bank? CED alternative strategies look at ways and means to "tether the loose foot of capital."[13]

Building community cohesion and skills is important to anyone who does CED work. They develop a core of people who want to be involved and then ask, what can we do? Could we intentionally create some networks to test various options? How do we link people to information and ideas? What are potential job generators in addition to housing and services? How can one project support another?

The following are examples of successful, large scale, interlocking CED activities: Foodshare in Toronto, Neechi Foods in Winnipeg and the Evangeline Cooperative Movement in PEI.

Foodshare Toronto started in 1985, with municipal and United Way funding, to coordinate emergency food services. It has expanded to be involved with the entire food system. Its website[14] states: "We see hunger as just one symptom of a food system that is geared to treating food primarily as a commodity…. We try to promote an awareness that fresh, whole foods are key to health, well-being and disease prevention, and to illustrate this principle through all our programs." Foodshare is involved in "grassroots program delivery, advocacy for social assistance reform, job creation and training, nutrition education, farmland preservation and campaigns for comprehensive food labelling." With grants from governments, Foodshare runs a Good Food Box that reaches thousands of people, undertakes roof-top gardening, has catering cooperatives and a nutrition in the schools program. Its Field to Table program creates and maintains partnerships with local farmers and food suppliers. It runs an online toolkit to help people start their own food security program.

Neechi Foods Coop is an Aboriginal, worker-owned, cooperative retail store in north end Winnipeg, which is dedicated to building a self-reliant economy based on the goods and services consumed in the community. When supermarkets abandoned the inner city, Neechi Foods organized in the late 1980s to meet inner city needs: buying and hiring locally. It is still thriving today. Neechi Foods is part of a diverse and successful web of CED activities in Manitoba, which includes the Assiniboine Credit Union and a number of locally owned and controlled financial institutions, CED delivery agencies and housing non-profits and cooperatives.[15] Its principles have even been adopted by the CED program of the government of Manitoba.

The Evangeline region, in the Acadian area of Prince Edward Island, is home to a network of cooperatives that includes a credit union, grocery stores, housing developments, fishing cooperatives, a community pasture, a funeral home and a cable distribution company. "The Conseil de développement coopératif represents 14 co-ops that have a combined total of 7,435 members and 233 employees. These cooperatives own assets worth $66 million."[16]

The Informal, Underground or Invisible Economy

Gertrude McIntyre writes:

> Through years of economic decline, unemployment and high taxes, the people of Glace Bay learned their own set of economic survival tools. Their tools encompass a variety of overt and covert activities of exchange and trade. They make up the informal economy.[17]

A whole other economy, invisible to the state economy, is called the "informal economy." It includes everything from the work of the family and reproduction, unpaid domestic services like child care and elder care, to sharing garden produce, home-made beer, wild game and kitchen production, flea markets, volunteer activities for the public good and barter. It also includes activities that are transacted in money but are conducted outside the acknowledged economy, such as illegal activities and work done "under the table" — cash transactions for renovations as well as prostitution, backroom gambling, informal lotteries and drug trafficking.

The government criminalizes many informal economy activities in its quest for tax revenues. In the case of drug production and trafficking, there are strong reasons for all of us to want more control over it. However, the government attack on the informal economy cuts off morally acceptable barter and exchange and unduly criminalizes impoverished people. For example, when an ice road that has been used by northerners for generations is declared to be a recognized public road, it forces First Nations people to buy unaffordable insurance and licences for vehicles which they previously were able to operate without these costs.[18] When we tried to establish a barter system in Sudbury, many of the tradespeople who wanted to join it were unable to because they would risk having to pay taxes they could not afford on bartered services.

Grassroots Economic Opportunity Development and Evaluation (GE-ODE) in Sudbury was set up to stimulate the legal aspects of the informal economy. We established a barter system, a Good Food Box (to distribute local organic food to families), a community van and a number of community gardens, all of which operated outside the currency economy. The following are examples of other activities that share living and working experiences but do not require setting up an entire institution:

- group-living experiences: camping, retreats, shared parenting, training sessions;
- sharing meals on a regular or occasional basis, including preparation, cleanup and planning;
- setting up a childcare exchange or a playgroup;
- building bees, cleaning bees, quilting, etc.

To some extent, CED activity may expropriate mutual aid and barter in the informal and the subsistence economy into the wage economy. For example, caring for children and the elderly, producing food stuffs at home, changing tires on the car and driving neighbours or family members around are usually carried on without exchanging money. Transforming these relationships into a money exchange may not be "progress" at all, but may do damage to the fragile social fabric of the community.

Notes

1. Barbara Brandt, *Whole Life Economics* (Gabriola Island, BC: New Society Publishers, 1995) p. 1.
2. <http://www.socialeconomyhub.ca/hub/>.
3. <www.honorearth.org>.
4. From my own files.
5. Bill McKibben, *Deep Economy: The Wealth of Communities and the Durable Future* (New York: Holt Paperback, 2007) p. 27.
6. Bill McKibben, *Deep Economy.*
7. The website <paecon.net> contains an English translation of their manifesto.
8. David Bollier, "Reclaiming the Commons: Why We Need to Protect Our Public Resources from Private Encroachment," *Boston Review* 2003 <http://bostonreview.net/BR27.3/bollier.html>.
9. Asha Krishnakumar, "Farmers Battle for Seed Rights," *Frontline* 20, 15, (July 19–August 01) 2003 <http://www.hinduonnet.com/fline/fl2015/stories/20030801000808000.htm>.
10. Kim Zalent, *Economic Home Cooking: An Action Guide for Congregation on Community Economic Development* (Chicago: Community Workshop on Economic Development, 1988) p. 5
11. Mario Polese and Richard Sheamur, *The Periphery in the Knowledge Economy: The Spatial Dynamics of the Canadian Economy and the Future of the Non-Metropolitan Regions in Quebec and the Atlantic Provinces* (Moncton, NB: The Canadian Institute for Research on Regional Development, 2003).
12. Canada-Ontario Business Service Centre, "Small Business Highlights," 2009. Downloaded October 10, 2009 from <http://www.canadabusiness.ca/servlet/ContentServer?cid=1184872136879&pagename=CBSC_ON/CBSC_WebPage/CBSC_WebPage_Temp&lang=en&c=CBSC_WebPage>
13. Gertrude Anne MacIntyre, *The Third Option: Linking Top-down and Bottom-up Efforts in Community-Based Development* (Sydney, NS: University College of Cape Breton, 2002).

14. Foodshare website <www.foodshare.net>.
15. John Loxley, Jim Silver and Kathleen Sexsmith (eds.), "The State of Economic Development in Winnipeg," in John Loxley, Kathleen Sexsmith and Jim Silver, *Doing Community Economic Development* (Halifax: Fernwood Publishing and Canadian Centre for Policy Alternatives, 2007).
16. Le Conseil de Développement Coopératif, n.d., "The World Capital of Co-operation: A Bit of History on the Evangeline Co-operative Movement" <http://www.conseilcoopipe.org/Histoire.cfm?Lang=EN&CalendarID=1>.
17. Gertrude Anne MacIntyre, *The Third Option*, p. 159.
18. From my files on the Victor Mine Project in northern Ontario.

10

Looking After Our Physical Needs

This chapter looks at three of the ways that activists are meeting our physical needs while building our own institutions, creating authentic relationships and shifting our culture: reclaiming our food system from the multi-nationals, ensuring green and affordable housing and dealing with our wastes.

Reclaiming the Food System

The United Nations Food and Agriculture Organization estimated in June 2009 that 1.2 billion people were going hungry every day and that this was caused — not by a lack of food — but by increasing impoverishment (and concentration of wealth) and by rising food prices. In Canada, Hungercount2009 states that 794,738 people used a food bank in March 2009, an increase of 18 percent from the year before. Of food bank users, 37 percent were children. and half of those helped were families with children.[1] In a country of 33 million people, this is unacceptable. In addition, the way we produce our food is not sustainable. Prevalent practices destroy the soil, pollute the water and air, and produce luxury foods for the wealthy at the expense of subsistence livelihoods for everyone. We rely on chemicals — many of them toxic — and transnational distribution networks to feed ourselves. The companies that run the food industry put profits before feeding people with practices like genetically modified crops and "terminator" seeds (which depend on chemicals to grow and cannot reproduce themselves). In answer to these twin concerns: hunger and the effects of the current food system on health and the environment, a movement for food security has emerged in Canada and around the world.

The food security movement brings together creative ideas and activities for reclaiming the food economy, locally and globally. Based on ensuring the provision of healthy and plentiful food to all, the movement has all sorts of opportunities for exciting and inventive organizing, ranging from gardening to massive protests about the political economy of food. Working on food issues quickly pulls people into one of the most creative and widespread aspects of the global justice movement.

We all spend lots of money on food. In most Canadian cities, the majority of that money goes to a few giant corporations. They own most of the "independents" too, although it may appear that we are shopping somewhere else. Every seller in the food distribution chain increases the eventual price to the consumer. Since Brewster Kneen wrote *From Land to Mouth* in 1989, awareness about the high transportation costs of the supermarket food we eat has resulted in a strong "eat local" movement. Farmers markets, community shared agriculture, buyers clubs, community gardens and food cooperatives attempt to eliminate wholesalers and cut down on the amount of the food dollar that goes toward energy costs, fertilizers and pesticides, packaging and advertising.

There is also a growing awareness of the power of transnational corporations in controlling the food system, and a determination to build "food sovereignty" — peoples' control — as the basis of food security and environmental sustainability. The *Peoples' Food Policy Project*[2] is engaging the Canadian public in a participatory process to tell stories about reclaiming the food system and developing a food sovereignty policy for Canada.

Food Secure Canada (FSC) is a Canadian organization that works to unite people and groups working for food security nationally and globally.[3] Their website says:

> FSC works to ensure that the following interconnected goals are achieved:
>
> *Zero Hunger*: All people at all times must be able to acquire, in a dignified manner, adequate quantity and quality of culturally and personally acceptable food.
>
> *A sustainable food system* (including the fishery and other wild foods): Food in Canada must be harvested, produced, processed, distributed and consumed in a manner which maintains and enhances the quality of land, air and water for future generations, and in which people are able to earn a living wage in a safe and healthy working environment by harvesting, growing, producing, processing, handling, retailing and serving food.
>
> *Healthy and safe food*: Nourishing foods must be readily at hand (and less nourishing ones restricted); food (including wild foods) must not be contaminated with pathogens or industrial chemicals; and no novel food can be allowed to enter the environment or food chain without rigorous independent testing and the existence of an on-going tracking and surveillance system, to ensure its safety for human consumption.

There are many different approaches to reclaiming our food, beginning with our own gardens. When we create organic vegetable gardens, converting lawns to food, share produce with our neighbours and preserve the rest, we are making a contribution to changing the world we live in. If we help create community gardens on vacant land, we do more.

Urban Gardens

In the Downtown Eastside of Vancouver, a beautiful urban community garden shows off the ethnic diversity of the neighbourhood and allows even the poorest street person to garden if they wish. Many municipalities have composting programs; in some cities this is being extended to create garden plots. Wild flowers and wild spaces are more ecologically sound than lawns and parks with well-tended grass. Roof-top gardening is growing in most Canadian cities. The conversion by local people of disaster zones in places like downtown Detroit and post-Katrina New Orleans to urban agriculture are stunning examples.

Buyers Clubs

Once a week, or less often, buyers club members get together to agree on an order: so many pounds of flour, sugar, so many tins of tomatoes. One of the members takes responsibility for purchasing these goods at bulk rates from the wholesalers or producers, and then the other members come to their house to pay for the goods and pick them up. Sophisticated buyers clubs have refrigerators, good sources of organic produce and so on. Food cooperatives are large buyers clubs. Many of them find themselves in competition with supermarkets, and unless there is real member loyalty, they are unable to compete. Some of them, trying to cut costs for their members, end up exploiting their own labour.

Farmers Markets

Farmers markets provide an opportunity for local producers to sell their produce and for consumers to purchase directly from them. They provide not only good food but an opportunity to create innovative social relationships. The farmers market movement is growing exponentially in Canada. A study released by Farmers Markets Canada in February 2009 states that the impact of farmers markets on the Canadian economy in 2008 was $3.09 billion.[4]

Farmers markets often work best when they are only open one or two days a week, as the market coincides with the busiest season on the farm, and most farmers cannot afford either staff for the market or the rental for an all-week or all year facility. A time-limited occasional market can also gain the support of local food merchants because they don't see it as competition.

Persuading a supermarket to stock organic locally grown produce is also a strategy for obtaining local food. Most supermarkets do not want to source locally as they demand "dependable" large quantities, which are difficult for most small farmers to provide. As well, the ever-available foods delink the supermarket consumer from an awareness of the cyclical nature of the growing season. Farmers markets, on the other hand, educate their consumers to the seasonal availability of food

Community Shared Agriculture

Community Shared Agriculture (CSA) links the farmer with the consumer in "an environmentally just way."[5] A direct link is set up between a specific group of consumers and one or more farmers to address two main problems: farmers bearing all the risks in food production and consumers needing more awareness about the source of their food. In return for a weekly basket filled with whatever is harvestable at that time, most CSA farmers have members pay a lump sum in advance for a share in the season's harvest, although some prefer to work on a pay-as-you-order basis.[6] Models range from purely subscription service CSAs to projects where the consumers actively participate in the physical labour of planting, weeding and harvesting. Most CSAs also depend on short-term hiring and non-member volunteer labour contributions. When members contribute, they help in harvesting, distribution and outreach. Although having members experience the farm firsthand is part of the idea behind CSA, many of the farmers find that this requires a lot of their energy to organize.

Seed Saving

Seed saving is another significant strategy arising from the need to undermine monoculture and to preserve and increase the diversity of plant genetic stock. In Canada, Seeds of Diversity[7] advocates for seed diversity, puts out a magazine (online) and runs events like "seedy Saturdays," where gardeners exchange their seeds and purchase from small, independent seed growers.

Forest Foods

Foods from the forest are referred to as non-timber forest products by the industrial world, but they include mushrooms, vegetables, berries, fruits and teas that grow in the woods. Forestry practices that destroy this resource are being challenged by Aboriginal people, environmental groups and the Canadian Paperworkers' Union, among others. Timber management plans that include selective cutting, proper reforestation, the preservation of old growth areas and wetlands, and biological diversity are possible and available. Projects also include tree planting projects in rural and urban areas, the creation of wind breaks and protection of wetlands and green spaces.

Fishers, Trappers and Hunters

Michael Harris in *Lament for an Ocean* writes:

> The last Beothuk Indian died in Newfoundland in 1829. The Great
> Auk, a flightless bird that once lived in profusions on Funk Island,
> was hunted to extinction in 1852. The last Newfoundland wolf died
> in 1930. Schools of haddock 150 miles long and 25 miles wide once
> lived on the Grand Banks and the St. Pierre Bank. The Soviets and
> the Spanish lined up their factory-freezers for miles and took the
> spawning stock. In five years, the haddock was gone.[8]

For millennia, the management of the fish, animals and birds that
nourished communities was in the hands of the local people who harvested
them. The hunters, fishers and trappers were (and are) the experts about
these creatures — their patterns of birth, mating, caring for their young
and nutritional needs. Colonization drove the initial destruction of buffalo,
passenger pigeons and woodland caribou. Such devastating practices have
been continued in the fishery and wildlife management of governments in
Canada, which are driven not by sustainability, but by dollar-based economics
and the demands of large industries for privatization, land and access to the
resources. In recent decades, we have seen the total collapse of the cod stocks
on the East Coast in the 1980s, the impending destruction of the salmon in
British Columbia, a huge decline in the Lake Winnipeg commercial fishery,
a 90 percent decline of caribou herds in the Northwest Territories and
northern Quebec/Labrador, and enormous reduction in the Boreal song-
bird population. A number of Indigenous and community organizations and
networks are engaged in re-asserting local management of the harvesting of
wild creatures.

Fair Trade

Equiterre, a Quebec-based organization dedicated to socially and environmentally responsible choices, has produced the *Action Guidebook for Fair Trade*,
which tells us exactly how to go about organizing in this area.

> The development of fairer exchanges between Northern countries
> and Southern countries is essential to better the living conditions
> of millions of farmers and workers and is a way for us, citizens and
> consumers, to have a concrete impact to help develop international
> solidarity. Fair Trade can be defined as a system of economic ex-
> changes that respects the environment and workers' rights.... If,
> tomorrow morning, every student from these CEGEPs and universities
> woke up and sipped a cup of Fair Trade coffee, it would represent
> over 11,400 pounds of this coffee. For the members of a cooperative

from South America, this would represent over 115 pairs of shoes, 34 rooftops, 358 dental consultations, 238 shirts, 400 chickens or 2043 bus tickets to go into town, and this could be accomplished in a single morning! Imagine the impact in an entire lifetime! [9]

The increased popularity of fair trade has drawn supermarket chain stores and trans-nationals like Starbucks into the act. This raises three serious questions about fair trade as an alternative.

- Why farmers should produce for luxury markets in the North?
- Who are the intermediary organizations and to what extent do the proceeds from sales of the final product reach the producers in the Global South?
- How useful is this strategy when companies like Starbucks purchase a small percentage of fair trade products to pull in consumers but leave the bulk of their business unchanged?

Fighting Politically

As important as hands-on projects, however, is the political fight to reclaim our food system from the multinationals that control it. There are increasing numbers of organizations and groups that focus the concerns of local groups in order to change the laws and policy governing agriculture, food and fisheries. These include Food Secure Canada, the National Farmers Union, GRAIN, Canadian Organic Growers, the Living Oceans Society and various provincial and municipal food policy councils. They depend for their political clout on the networks and mobilized citizens working in their own communities around the world.

Providing Shelter

Like working on food issues, working on how we shelter ourselves brings up questions of distribution, justice, conservation, green technologies and sustainability. Currently, most of our housing system is based on the concept of private property and the rights of owners and developers to do what they want with their property. Even the rights of tenants to some security of tenure have had to be obtained through years of power struggles. Our system is inefficient, uses excessive amounts of energy, causes urban sprawl and is hard on the environment. Most importantly it relegates some people to slums and a few to mansions. It does not work. The movement for equitable housing in Canada and around the world has a number of aspects. Some of them are described below.

Non-Profit and Cooperative Housing

When five of us (plus our children) decided to buy an enormous old house in 1981, it cost us $47,000 plus the lawyer's fees. When we had to renegotiate the mortgage a year later, however, the interest rates had sky-rocketed to 22.75 percent. The credit union re-valued the house lower than the purchase price, so we had to take out a loan for the balance at an even higher rate of interest. To pay the doubled costs of living there, we took in more people. Suddenly there were twelve people living and eating and sleeping in that house instead of seven. The emotional intensity increased exponentially.

On the other hand, while everyone else we knew was losing their homes, we kept ours because we were willing to share it. When the willow tree ate the sewer line, and the roof started to leak like a sieve, we had a lot more hands to repair it. The kids grew up with an extended family, even if I did tend to scream at them all every morning as they poked around getting ready for school. For fifteen years that house provided a beautiful home with a garden and a swing and a crab-apple tree that blooms every spring. And my children and I have an extended family that still enriches our lives years after we have moved on — all for a shelter cost of less than $200 a month each. How do you beat that?

In Canada there are many examples of collective houses, co-housing, cooperative and non-profit housing developments. In August 2009, the Co-operative Housing Federation of Canada reported:

> For over 40 years, Canada's non-profit co-op housing sector has played an important role in creating more than 93,000 permanent affordable homes for over a quarter of a million Canadians in every province and territory across the country. Approximately 40 percent of these homes use federal or provincial assistance to help pay their housing charges, which are set at affordable levels according to household incomes. Other households pay the market rent. Canada's 2,200 non-profit housing co-operatives have also created strong, inclusive, self-directed mixed-income communities that promote positive social values and build families.[10]

Cooperatives are usually individual housing units that are owned in common by all the occupants, and managed by an elected board comprised of those occupants. The rents are determined by the costs, although most cooperatives can subsidize some units for members who cannot afford full market rent. One Charlottetown cooperative purchased an entire block of older row housing and rehabilitated it. They turned the centre of the block into a beautiful and useful landscaped common space.

Non-profit housing has the same range of options, but it is owned by a non-share capital corporation. Although tenants can have representation on the board or participate in a tenant management committee, the board of the corporation is legally responsible for all contracts and so on. If most of the units are to be rent-geared-to-income, or occupants don't want to be owners, this may be the only way to get funding. Some church properties have been converted to non-profit housing for the elderly or low-income people.

Most cooperatives and non-profits have some support from the federal and provincial governments (usually the result of a lengthy and prolonged political work) so that they can subsidize low-income neighbours. The cooperatives vary greatly from province to province, but one thing they do have in common is complex paperwork to get off the ground. If a person is interested in pursuing this area, they would be well-advised to seek the help of a resource group like the Cooperative Housing Federation and/or their members.

Provided the proposition is viable, private funding can be sought to establish cooperative housing from regular financial institutions, alternative investment funds and many churches and unions. Options open to church groups include financing through remortgaging church property, selling air rights and providing office and administrative help. Homes First Society in Toronto, Communitas in Edmonton and the Downtown Eastside Residents Association in Vancouver are organizations that have been successful, not only in building housing for homeless people, but in influencing government policy to be more responsive. More information about housing cooperatives and non-profits can be obtained from the Cooperative Housing Federation of Canada.[11]

Building and renovating housing can provide real opportunities to create jobs and provide training for community members. Projects in Winnipeg have excelled at this, although not without considerable challenges. Detailed information is contained in a research study undertaken as part of Manitoba Research Alliance on Community Economic Development.[12]

Green Housing

Efforts in the area of green housing are generally more concerned with environmental issues than distribution. The website of Low Impact Housing has links to resources.[13] There are a number of creative options, including:

- getting off the energy grid with passive and active solar, geo-thermal and wind power;
- applying energy conservation measures like retrofits;
- building homes with recycled materials;
- ending urban sprawl, with revised city planning;
- using grey water re-cycling and closed-loop waste systems; and
- limiting water consumption through revised plumbing schemes and no-water landscapes.

Healing the Land: Waste and Toxics

There is no away. Throwing out garbage, putting it by the curb, taking it to the dump — try as we might, we can never really make garbage disappear. When we throw garbage "away," it just goes somewhere else. We bury most of our garbage in landfills where it may stay forever. We burn some trash, but burning can pollute the air if not properly controlled, and it still leaves ash to bury. We can recycle many things, but even these processes require energy, and create waste and pollution.[14]

We have been using the natural world as an unending garbage dump for all our wastes: chemical wastes, mine tailings, oil sands tailings, municipal waste, sewage. We are nearing the carrying capacity of the planet, and we have to find ways, not only to limit the wastes we create, but to heal those areas that have been damaged and to contain in perpetuity those that cannot be fixed. We can come at these issues from a few different directions: reduced use and conservation, recycling and remediation.

Waste services that protect the planet cannot be carried out by individuals and local communities alone. Although there are a number of things we can do in our neighbourhoods, proper management of waste is a government responsibility. The danger in organizing around this cause is that it easily becomes a "not in my backyard" issue, when in fact, we need to change law and policies so that no one has to live with the dangers of toxins.

Reduced Use and Conservation

Producing two gold wedding bands leaves behind 6–50 tonnes of waste rock and tailings, most of which will be toxic forever.[15] Respecting the tremendous cost of producing gold jewellery would mean recycling those rings for many generations, as many people already do. Other metals leave behind similar messes, which often have to be managed at taxpayers' expense.

A big part of any sustainable economy is reducing the use of non-renewable energy, metals, plastics and other resources. Not only does this mean limiting personal consumption, but it is about changing government policies and regulations, such as a tax system that provides greater incentives to the mining of virgin materials than to the recycling of metals.

Recycling

There are an almost endless number of waste recycling projects that are available to community groups. One of the most sophisticated in Canada is United We Can in the Downtown Eastside of Vancouver. Started as a project to provide income for "dumpster divers," United We Can purchases plastic and glass bottles from street people and creates businesses with the income. Other ideas include:

- flea markets, rummage sales, secondhand stores;
- automobile recycling. Although this has gone on informally in poor communities since the invention of the automobile, a group of laid-off mechanics in Lethbridge are trying to turn it into a business. Old cars are taken apart and completely rebuilt, and then resold to the public at considerably less than the cost of a new car;
- community composting (in many cities now, the municipality has taken this on);
- paper, glass, rubber and plastic recycling; and
- libraries of useful objects: tools, bicycles, skates, skis, toys, fancy clothes. In Sudbury, the teenage street kids who ran the Do-Drop-Inn went to the police and asked them to give them the bicycles that they were going to auction off that spring. With these bicycles, they ran a "bicycle library" for the summer. Bikes were loaned out to kids and kept in repair by the teenagers.

Remediation: Understanding Risk Assessment

Many communities have been involved in fights over waste disposal: from nuclear waste facilities to the location of new garbage dumps to cleaning up toxic waste. Organizing around these issues is difficult for a number of reasons. People are worried that their property values will be affected when the news gets out. No one wants to think they have been poisoning their children. Facing the possibility of having to manage huge toxic sites "in perpetuity" is depressing and mind-boggling.

Government and industry will use "risk assessments" to minimize the danger and the costs of clean up. The language of risk assessment is a specialized language, often difficult for lay people to penetrate. Risk assessments of toxins are mathematical exercises, based on well over one hundred different assumptions. A change in any one of these assumptions can have a dramatic effect on the risk estimate. The modelling is rarely "ground-truthed" — with testing of human or animal tissue to see if it makes sense in the real world. Usually key information needed for an adequate assessment of effects is missing.

If the community is faced with a risk assessment, get help. Information and help is available from a variety of organizations, including the U.S.-based Center for Health and Environmental Justice, begun by Lois Gibbs.[16]

Notes

1. Food Banks Canada, *Hungercount 2009: A Comprehensive Report on Hunger and Food Bank Use in Canada and Recommendations for Change.* <http://foodbankscanada.ca/

main2.cfm?id=107185CB-B6A7-8AA0-6FE6B5477106193A>.

2. Peoples Food Policy Project website <peoplesfoodpolicy.ca>.
3. Food Secure Canada website <foodsecurecanada.org>.
4. Farmers Markets Canada website <Farmersmarketscanada.ca>.
5. Kreesta Doucette and Glen Koroluk, "Manitoba Alternative Food Production and Farm Marketing Models," in John Loxley, Kathleen Sexsmith and Jim Silver, *Doing Community Economic Development* (Halifax: Fernwood Publishing and Canadian Centre for Policy Alternatives, 2007) p. 172–73
6. Amunda Salm, "Eight Tips from the Experts to Make Your Community Shared Agriculture Project a Success," 1997 <http://eap.mcgill.ca/MagRack/COG/COG_E_97_04.htm>.
7. Seeds of Diversity website <http://www.seeds.ca/>.
8. Michael Harris, *Lament for an Ocean: The Collapse of the Atlantic Cod Fishery: A True Crime Story* (Toronto: McClelland and Stewart, 1998) p. 332.
9. Equiterre, *Action Guidebook for Fair Trade.* Montreal, 2006. <http://www.artisan-connect.net/documents.php?documentid=7008>.
10. Co-operative Housing Federation of Canada, "Non-Profit Co-operative Housing: Working to Safeguard Canada's Affordable Housing Stock for Present and Future Generations," submission to the 2009 Pre-Budget Consultations, August. <http://www.chfcanada.coop/eng/pdf/PublicPolicyDocs/Brief2009Pre-BudgetConsultations.pdf>
11. Cooperative Housing Federation of Canada website <http://www.chfc.ca/>.
12. Ian Skelton, Cheryl Selig and Lawrence Deane, "CED and Social Housing Initiatives in Inner-City Winnipeg," in John Loxley, Kathleen Sexsmith and Jim Silver, *Doing Community Economic Development* (Halifax: Fernwood Publishing and Canadian Centre for Policy Alternatives, 2007).
13. <http://lowimpacthousing.com/housing/resources.htm>.
14. The Rotten Truth website was created in 1998 by the Association of Science-Technology Centers Incorporated and the Smithsonian Institution Traveling Exhibition Service. <http://www.astc.org/exhibitions/rotten/away.htm>.
15. The No Dirty Gold campaign website <www.nodirtygold.org>.
16. <www.chej.org>.

11

Our Working Lives

I believe we honour each other with our daily work.
Everything I touch arrives in my hand
As a gift to me, no matter what its price
Having gotten here through so much labor and so many lives
That no one can truly affix a value.
And I also pass on what I do: meaning to honour others
By my life and work each day.
—Tom Wayman[1]

Our lives are made possible by the daily labour of millions of people around the globe who produce and distribute the food we eat, provide shelter, warmth, clothing and communications, remove wastes, care for one children and the elders, establish order. We do what we can for ourselves, and we sell our time and effort to employers. Because it consumes so much of our time and creativity, the way in which we earn our living changes how we look at and act in the world outside the job.

For most of my life, I have not been paid to be a community organizer. Instead, like lots of other people, I've had to do "real work." I've worked as a nurse's aide, a secretary, a bankteller, a research assistant, a service representative for the telephone company, a sales clerk, a teacher, a sod-layer, a gardener and a community legal worker.

Working as a bank teller made me very aware of the differences in income between people who came in as customers. I worried about my appearance a lot. I became very careful with money and receipts and bills.

Laying sod made me physically strong and tough, and, because the wages were so low, I was constantly worried about money. Loafing behind the boss's back became a game we played to get some needed breaks and self-respect.

Working at the legal clinic, where every client I saw was impoverished, desperate and facing a terrible life crisis of one sort or another — cut off from welfare, eviction, work injuries — turned me into a chronic worrier. I began to see our lives as very fragile indeed. And I became a passionate and effective advocate for the underdog everywhere I went.

In all these jobs, there were common threads. I like work most when I am learning something new, where I have room for individual initiative, where I enjoy my co-workers and where my labour is socially useful. These certainly aren't the characteristics of most jobs.

When I worked at Bell Canada from 1971 to 1973, I simply couldn't understand why anyone would organize work in that way. So I decided to find out, and in 1979 I put what I learned into *The Phone Book: Working at Bell Canada*.[2] What I learned was this:

Work is organized by the people who own the means of production. Their only interest in the work we all do is to get as much production out of us as possible at the least cost. Over the years the owners have tried out many different ways to organize and plan production, but the way that gives the most control to them and costs them the least has the following three characteristics:

- Jobs are divided into two basic categories. The owners and upper management do the intellectual planning functions, and the workers do the manual, clerical and repetitive functions.
- Decision-making is hierarchical. Structures can be rearranged and policies implemented easily from the top of the pyramid, but at the bottom of the pyramid there is only very limited movement possible.
- Every job is divided into its component parts; each part is given to a different detail worker and has a different rate of pay and status assigned to it.

The organization of work at Bell Canada provided a fine example of this system, which has not really changed at most large workplaces in over thirty years.

This idea, of labour being strictly divided into its component parts, was first postulated by a man named Charles Babbage in 1832. Basic to Babbage's then-novel conception of work was the division of a skill or craft into each of its separate parts and the assignment of each part to a different "detail worker." Before Babbage's time, each worker would perform all aspects of a task, just as a skilled cabinetmaker creates a whole piece of furniture. While workers might divide a process among themselves for the sake of efficiency, they would never willingly convert themselves into lifelong detail workers.

Even during Babbage's time, many workers retained the skills necessary to control their work. But new management practices in the first decades of the twentieth century were to change this. Frederick Winslow Taylor was the chief theoretician of the new management style. Its goal was to obtain the maximum possible production from employees in the shortest possible time. It was carried out by relieving employees of all "unnecessary" information about their work and concentrating information in the hands of management. Management could then use its resulting monopoly over knowledge to parcel out the work and control each step of the labour process. Taylor believed that the greatest obstacle to production was the loafing, or "soldiering," that workers did on the job and that the most destructive impulse was "systematic soldiering" — the deliberate effort on the part of workers to conceal just how fast the work could be done. Taylor's ideas were eagerly embraced and implemented by the two men who had perhaps the greatest impact on modern workplace design in the world: Henry Ford and V.I. Lenin.

For workers involved in this process, it was a direct assault on their autonomy and dignity, an assault that was intensified later by the ability of companies to monitor employee productivity electronically. Detail work and scientific management have now become the basis of the organization of work in advanced industrial countries. Despite talk of job enrichment and team planning, the decisions about the organization of work, product, ownership and control are retained by the owners and managers of the corporation.

The decision-making process — centralized in management — is mystified and imbues the managers with an aura of competence. Workers at the bottom of the pyramid feel unable to understand or challenge the direction or operations of the corporation. Life-long detail work and rigorous on-the-job discipline cause employees to see themselves as incompetent and ignorant. It undermines the confidence of workers who do the repetitive and low-paid jobs. It divides workers from one another, through differences in wages and status. The hierarchy of skills and status carries over into employees' social acceptance of one another. Although computer-based technologies have had dramatic impacts on work — the use of robotics, globalized and just-in-time production, the elimination of many semi-skilled and repetitive jobs — it has not changed the basic organization of the workplace; nor has it provided workers with more control over what they produce, how they produce it or how it is distributed. Most of us are still wage slaves.

Workplaces are not at all democratic, and in non-union workplaces the power of an employer on the shop floor is absolute. Any worker can be expelled from a workplace for "disruptive" behaviour. Even in such benign workplaces as churches, fired employees are routinely told of their termination in a supervisor's office and escorted out of the building without being allowed to say goodbye to fellow workers.

In the last thirty years, work has increasingly become part-time and contractual, with many workers holding more than one job just to stay alive. Many large companies have carried out "redundancy programs," which have laid off huge numbers of their workers, attempting to replace them with computer technologies or through "leaner" methods. Companies have also removed many middle management positions ("de-layering"). Others have shipped work offshore to India, China and Mexico. During the two decades of massive globalization, the global division between those who have and those who have not has increased exponentially.[3]

We do our community organizing with many people who spend at least thirty-five hours of their week in hierarchical and rigid environments. Today, most government and non-profit groups are organized on this model. Sometimes we even inadvertently set it up in our own organizations. If we wonder why tellers, service representatives and frontline civil servants seem uncaring, we have to look no further than the structure in which they work. Daily, workers are only "following orders" when they continue to carry out work that destroys the environment or builds military equipment or makes others suffer. Any responsibility they feel for the eventual products of their labour has been taken from them long ago.

It has to be the work of community and labour organizers to re-awaken a sense of responsibility to the larger world within those of us who are "just doing our job," to enable the agency of working people to shape their lives on and off the job: to support the whistle-blowers, the brown-envelope passers, the courage of people who refuse to do destructive work for the elites and who find ways to support and create social and environmental justice within the places that employ them.

Trade Unions and Legalized Bargaining

In recent years, corporations have waged a concerted attack on trade unions. In 2007, the percentage of unionized employees in Canada was only around 30 percent of non-agricultural paid employment,[4] down about 2.5 percent from ten years before.

Workers sought collective bargaining for years as a way of gaining control over the conditions and rates of their work. When collective bargaining was legalized during the Second World War because employers needed a secure and stable labour force, workers discovered that the victory was partial indeed.[5] They could only strike when the contract expired, and in between had to discipline their members if they took matters into their own hands. The negotiations and grievance procedure transformed trade union leaders from militant shop floor stewards to lawyers who haggle with management over the dollars their members will receive for the sale of their labour. What is produced, how it is produced and how it is distributed are considered to be "management rights," beyond the scope of the labour contract. A lack of understanding about how this process works can lead to disillusionment and charges of "selling out" by rank-and-file unionists and activists.

The closed shop and the Rand formula granted security to recognized trade unions through enforcement of compulsory dues from their membership.[6] Although it has freed unions from the arduous work of recruiting members and collecting dues on a regular basis, in the long run, it has resulted (in some unions) in the leadership no longer really being accountable to the people who elect them. The Rand formula is now under attack, and unions are discovering that they may lose the ability to keep their membership and dues in place.

Unfortunately, legalized collective bargaining also keeps trade union boards and staff so occupied with technical detail and busy work that it becomes almost impossible to confront the power of management in any basic way. Although collective bargaining gives workers power to negotiate wages and conditions of work, it leaves the powers of management intact — powers to introduce new technologies, change products and move capital from one region to another. For this reason, strikes are often followed by plants closing or moving to Mexican *maquiladores*, or by the introduction of labour-saving or deskilling technologies. For this reason, health care workers, teachers and social service workers continuously see the quality and social utility of their jobs diminished but feel powerless to stop it. Trade unions in Canada are also limited in their abilities to organize with the unorganized (those who do not belong to unions) or to assist laid-off union members; they become protective of their own position of relative privilege vis-à-vis other workers.

Further, the legalistic and research skills required of union leadership in Canada create divisions between the rank-and-file and the leadership and the staff. Instead of encouraging the agency of workers, the union leadership increasingly fears rebellion in the ranks. Many working people in Canada have few models of truly democratic organization to draw from and so are not skilled at creating or running them. The upshot of all this is that, although unions are essential for the defence of workers' rights on the shop floor, they have been badly disorganized by the collective bargaining process. Reclaiming worker agency in the union means confronting not only the boss but the union executive and bureaucracy; it means organizing from below.

I don't want these comments to be misunderstood. Trade unions are essential to the defence of workers in Canada and elsewhere. I have worked in union and non-union shops. At least in the union shops we had freedom of speech and some protection against the arbitrariness of management. In non-union shops there was nothing. Most non-union workers owe whatever benefits they have to management's fear of a union coming in. If the trade union movement in Canada is allowed to fall apart, we will all suffer. The union struggle for internal democracy, relevance and survival is our struggle.

Strikes and Strike Support

Many legal strikes at workplaces are like going in to a formal battle and giving the opposition the time, date and method of attack. Strikes have become ritualized showings of support for bargaining demands, where the workers agree to withhold their labour from an employer until they get a decent contract. Although workers pay themselves strike pay out of their accumulated strike fund, they face serious financial hardship on a long strike. Much of this hardship is born by women, as they are usually responsible for trying to manage a reduced household budget and suffer the ire of creditors and the tensions of the family.

When strikes are in the public sector, it is the workers themselves and the people they serve that get hurt, not the employer. Bus strikes can become excuses to cut down on public transit. Strikes in the health sector penalize those who are ill. Strikes in schools and universities hurt the students. Garbage strikes endanger public well-being. The just demands of public sector workers for better wages and working conditions become a means for the corporate sector to make further inroads into the Commons; they increase the public sense that greed trumps service every time. We desperately need to resurrect alternatives to striking: work-ins, occupations, involving the community in leading the demands for better conditions for the people they depend on.

The bus drivers of Victoria and Vancouver won public support despite a thirteen-week service shut down. During a two-year campaign, the union emphasized service — refusing to implement service cuts, wearing costumes to work, producing "un-fare" cards and so on.

Successful strikes behave in ways that have not been anticipated by the employer:

- whenever the strike costs the employer substantially more than he saves on unpaid wages;
- when they last longer than the employer expected: the stockpile is used up, the competition starts to take over the market and so on;
- when the employer thought the workers would not strike and they did. "Wildcat" strikes are illegal in Canada. If the union leadership does not discipline the workers they can be held liable for damages to the company. However, because they are so rarely anticipated by the employer, they can be very effective;
- when the strike creates secondary pressure on the employer: from the community, its customers, or its shareholders, globally;
- when the strike starts to affect the value of company shares; and
- when the strike is used in conjunction with blockades, work-ins, or occupations.

Some unions and workers are gathering ideas for economic conversion to more socially useful production, to worker cooperatives, or healthier work, or more environmentally friendly workplaces. Some workers have access to information that could help the movement: statistics, documents, clients with similar problems, policies and plans that will affect the community. Sometimes just being an honest and caring person to the people we work with provides an example that is almost revolutionary.

Worker Cooperatives

Worker cooperatives are an alternative to the hierarchical structure of most workplaces. A worker cooperative is an enterprise that is owned and controlled by the workers. Decision-making is on a one-member-one-vote basis. No outside investors are permitted and no privileges for capital over labour are tolerated. Worker cooperatives provide an opportunity of workplace democracy. The only bosses are those chosen by and responsible to the workers in the enterprise.

Worker cooperatives have a better survival rate and higher productivity than other forms of business organization.[7] They make a valuable contribution to increased democracy at work and to the democratic structure of the country as a whole. They tend to be more responsive to the needs of the community in which they operate and to job satisfaction for the member-workers.

Worker cooperatives are often considered by workers as an alternative to plant closure. In Argentina and Venezuela, worker cooperative takeovers of industrial enterprises abandoned by their owners have become a key strategy in economic renewal. The film *The Take*, available from the National Film Board, provides a window on the creation of worker cooperatives in Argentina.[8]

One of the larger worker cooperatives in Canada is The Big Carrot (a health food retailer in Toronto). The Big Carrot opened in 1983, after the workers in a health food store decided to become a worker cooperative instead of being laid off. Their website says:

> As business grew, so did our worker owner membership. Presently there are over 60 worker owners. The Big Carrot is run the same democratic way it was 25 years ago. Full time staff are eligible to join our co-op after one full year of employment. After an initial investment is made (the same amount since 1983) as well as a $1.00 for a voting share, the member may then participate in committee work and attends membership meetings to discuss store policies, capital expenditures, voting in new members and general business operations. 70 percent of annual profits are shared by the members

119

based on the amount of labour hours worked. The rest goes back into the business with a percentage donated to other worker-co-ops, sustainable agriculture and the community. If a member decides to leave the co-op, they receive their initial investment back as well as any outstanding labour dividends. No member, at any time, may receive a portion of the net worth of the company.[9]

There is also a history of cooperative farms in Canada. In 1945, the Saskatchewan government encouraged the establishment of cooperative farms for returning war veterans. They were run democratically by their members just like any worker cooperative. One of these is the Matador Co-operative, which has been in existence for forty-two years.

Perhaps the most sophisticated worker cooperatives in the world are in the Basque Region of Spain, where the Mondragon Co-operative has been in existence since 1946. An interlocking set of worker cooperatives engaged in plastics, food production, training, medical care and a credit union now employ more than 25,000 people in over 150 enterprises.[10] There are a number of films and books on the Mondragon experiment.

Worker cooperatives in and of themselves do not guarantee social transformation: if the cooperative members are fascists, we will have a fascist cooperative. On the other hand, for those of us who want to do "good work" together, this is an ideal model. Hazel Corcoran, the executive director of the Canadian Worker Co-operative Federation, reported in February 2011:

> There are about 350 worker co-operatives in Canada employing over 13,000 people, with revenues of $470 million. An estimated two-thirds of worker cooperatives in Canada are located in Quebec, employing about 1,000 people. If we include the related types of co-ops (multi-stakeholder or solidarity co-ops, and worker-shareholder co-ops), then there are approximately 600 such cooperatives. There are several different federations of worker co-ops: the Canadian Worker Co-operative Federation is Canada-wide, including regional federation members in Quebec. Our regional federation members are le Réseau de la coopération du travail du Québec (Quebec Worker Co-operation Network), and la Fédération des coopératives forestières du Québec.[11]

Notes

1. Tom Wayman, "Interview 2: Ambiguity," *Free Time: Industrial Poems* (Toronto: MacMillan of Canada, 1977) p. 116.
2. Joan Kuyek, *The Phone Book: Working at Bell Canada* (Toronto: Between the Lines, 1979).
3. Franco Gandolfi, "The Mean and Lean Firm: The Latest in Reductions in Force

(RIF)," *Ivey Business Journal* January/February, 2009. <http://www.iveybusiness-journal.com/article.asp?intArticle_ID=803>.

4. Canada, *Human Resources and Social Development* website <http://www.hrsdc.gc.ca/eng/lp/wid/union_membership.shtml>.

5. For information on the history of trade unions in Canada, I have drawn on my own files and Pat Bird, *Of Dust and Time and Dreams and Agonies* (Willowdale, ON: John Deyell Company 1975); Walter Johnson, *The Trade Unions and the State* (Montreal: Black Rose Books, 1978); Robert Laxer, *Canada's Unions* (Toronto: James Lorimer, 1970); and Desmond Morton, *Working People* (Ottawa: Deneau and Greenberg, 1980).

6. The "closed shop" is a requirement in a collective agreement that requires all members of a bargaining unit to be union members in good standing. The "Rand formula" requires the employer to deduct the union dues from the wages of all employees in a bargaining unit, whether they are members of the union or not. The "bargaining unit" for workers in a company is determined by the Labour Relations Board or a similar body after negotiation with the union and the employer.

7. C. Axworthy, "Worker Co-operatives," address given April 4, 1986, Sudbury, Ontario.

8. Avi Lewis and Naomi Klein, *The Take* (film), Barnia-Alper Productions, Klein-Lewis Productions and the National Film Board, 2007.

9. The Big Carrot, "We Are a Worker Owner Co-op." <http://thebigcarrot.ca/index.php?id=6> downloaded September 22, 2009.

10. Their website is <http://www.mondragon-corporation.com/>.

11. Hazel Corcoran, executive director, CWCF/FCCT presentation to the federal Finance Committee, submission concerning the potential of worker cooperatives top meet the major challenges posed by the economic development of Canadian communities, Part II. February 15, 2011. <www.canadianworker.coop/>.

12

Paying the Bills for Social Change

Finding money to do social change work raises thorny questions about how we relate to the power structure and the people who work in it. Since most wealth is in the hands of the owners of transnational corporations or in the coffers of the governments that tax us, there is increasingly little for us to use for social change. Government cutbacks — demanded by the power elites — have meant that more of our energy goes into fundraising for health, education and other social services that should be supported by government funding: e.g., cancer treatment centres, transition houses, food banks and school recreation programs. The result is that social change groups compete with more socially acceptable causes in their campaigns for donors.

In addition, there are a number of government funding programs that have been developed by sympathetic public servants in response to public pressure. These cover areas such as training and apprenticeship, Indigenous well-being, childcare and education, eldercare and academic research. Such programs can provide funds for work we need and want to do in our communities. Most social change organizations cannot afford to ignore these programs; we need the dollars too much. However, they have their own logic, which will shape what we do.

Since the 1960s, corporate interests influencing the Canadian government have been extremely good at using funding to manipulate social change groups. A minimum wage salary is offered to a radical tenants group in return for their incorporating. Or a women's centre gets funding for special projects but not for work on reproductive rights. Or a group wants to hire staff for an unemployed help centre but can only do so using workfare dollars. As a result of the strings that are often attached to government funding, some organizations feel that we should not accept it for our work.

However, many progressives have a different take on government funding. We have not only lobbied government federally, provincially and municipally for programs that might benefit the local community, but we have been able to use the resulting granting programs to build our organizations. The resources of government — raised through taxing all of us — belong to the people of this land; we cannot abandon them to corporate interests.

We see the money from government as reparations for the damage done to our communities and ecosystems by harmful economic policies.

There are also possibilities for funding portions of our work from foundations, which are effectively tax shelters for the wealthy, or directly from corporations. Like funding from governments, these sources may require community groups to tailor certain activities to make them fit. Raising money from individuals through direct mail and donor campaigns are alternatives used by many larger organizations that have the "moral high-ground." There is an entire industry built up around donor cultivation and solicitation. Unless an organization has been around for a few decades and has a broad base of appeal, a large-scale donor campaign is unlikely to work. Most of us are inundated with appeals from worthy causes at a time when our real incomes are dropping: the result is a kind of "donor fatigue." Some organizations have wealthy patrons; however, it is unlikely that social change work will attract that kind of support. Membership fees also compete with other demands on individuals, as do community fundraising events.

So, what do we do? All groups have expenses, and few organizations that are engaged in radical social change are eligible for government and foundation grants or corporate help, unless they find a way to design a project and phrase their application to suit the program available. In other words, the source of funds will certainly influence the direction that the organization takes. Where we get our money is, therefore, a crucial matter. This chapter explores some of the contradictions this brings up.

Contradiction: Packaging Dissent

Battles between corporate and elite interests and the interests of the public are played out in government offices, in parliamentary committees, in the public service. There are a number of ways in which those who hold power attempt to manage dissent when it does break out. Canadian governments have become adept at managing rather than directly confronting or responding to dissent; and our government and corporations have exported these tools to other countries around the world. These management strategies become invisible to us over time, and many organizers become corrupted, co-opted or just lose their way. Anyone who wants to organize needs to understand how it works.

"You have to understand," the Ottawa mandarin said to me, "there are so many people to my right, that I like to have a few people on my left. It keeps me honest." The man who said this to me in 1965 was one of the architects of the Company of Young Canadians (CYC), established by the Pearson government in response to the demands of student activists and others for a radical redistribution of power in Canada. The CYC set up an organizing committee of concerned and pre-eminent citizens and hired a research team (mostly young and full of wishful thinking) in the summer of 1965. The CYC selected and funded projects from all over the country that were to hire young adults at very low rates of pay ("volunteers") to work for social change.[1]

From the beginning there was a struggle between what the activist leaders of the CYC wanted to do and what the elites and the government thought they should do. The leaders of the youth movement wanted opportunities for young people to live and work with marginalized people so that they could learn from each other and use their shared perceptions and skills to build new bases of power in Canada. This meant leaving the projects open and fluid so that they could take the path that the community people wanted them to take and having volunteer control of the administration of the CYC so it could respond to the needs of the field without establishment interference.

Government spokespeople always claimed that they were in favour of "community development," "empowerment" and so on. At first a number of the projects really did take on the establishment. Youth took over the streets of Yorkville. They organized with tenants and youth in Kingston. Rocky Jones worked with Black people in Nova Scotia. In Montreal, Calgary and many other cities, CYC volunteers really listened to the people in the neighbourhoods and began to build effective community groups. For most of the young people in the CYC it was an intensely radicalizing experience. For the local people it was an exciting time. For the entrenched local elites, it was a nightmare, and they began to demand controls over the CYC and any similar government programs.

In 1969, the conflicts came to a head over the CYC in Quebec, where a number of volunteers were said to be members of the Front du Liberation du Quebec (FLQ). The government's response was to appoint a controller, on the pretext that funds were being misused, and to change the criteria for projects and the administration of the CYC. The controller, Max Mendlesohn, was "a top-notch administrator and a highly competent manager. His forte was figures, plans, structures, job descriptions, and policies."[2] Within a few weeks, he delivered the CYC program firmly into the hands of the government. Shortly afterwards it was disbanded and followed by a range of other programs which were administered through the Job Creation Branch and the Secretary of State. These, too, became ways for people to fund work for community empowerment, but, as they were successful, new administrative controls were introduced that limited their effectiveness. These controls included the following:

- the requirement for a board of directors for local projects that represented a "variety of community interests" and did not include the staff of the project;

- money only available for special short-term projects, not for long-term funding, and criteria that shifted regularly;
- approval for projects from a member of Parliament or a committee established by him/her;
- determination of a goal/issue at the outset of a project including a "needs analysis" and "anticipated outcomes": a method which precluded an issue evolving out of the process of community consultation and action;
- the requirement for measurable results or outputs such as clientele, case files, job placements, etc. The system evolved into results-based management.[3]

A study by Roxana Ng of the evolution of an immigrant women's centre,[4] clearly shows how the imposition of these administrative procedures are used to control community work. The organization she studied had begun as a collective of immigrant women helping one another achieve justice and jobs. Once it sought state funding, it was required to have a board of directors, produce regular accounts and funding applications, and show measurable production (i.e., number of clients placed in jobs). It quickly was transformed into a service agency with a tiny staff and a large clientele, delivering a government program.

In the late sixties, advocacy for store-front legal clinics resulted in a number being established in Canada. Usually, they were staffed by a mixture of street-wise community people and progressive law students or lawyers who wanted to provide representation and advocacy for the poor. Sometimes they had a board or an advisory committee that was made up of leaders from the poor community, or the injured workers union, or some such militant organization. The advocacy took place in the context of this grassroots organizing.

When we first set up the Community Information Service in Kingston, for example, it did workshops for welfare recipients about their rights, and it was funded by private citizens, unions, churches and the local NDP riding association. Our mostly volunteer staff helped organize tenants for collective bargaining. It saw welfare recipients advocating for each other with the welfare department. It participated in running progressive candidates for municipal council. People who came in asking for help in a crisis were later recruited to help others with similar problems. We built a network of committed activists who helped one another; put out a community newspaper and pressured for change.

To some of the law students working in the clinic, it seemed like a good idea to have Queen's Law School take it over and use it as a means to train students. Although this provided a stable base of funding, the effect of the move was to completely dis-empower the community people who had worked there. All of a sudden, the skills the community people brought to the organization were perceived as "unsophisticated, too radical" and so on. Many of them did not understand the language that the lawyers used in the meetings and felt stupid when they had to ask for an explanation. They voted with their feet. Quite rapidly, the clinic ceased to get impoverished people in crisis together for mutual aid and became a service that called the welfare office to get cheques released, launched appeals in administrative tribunals and translated the poor person's situation into legalese or social worker jargon. Losing control of the clinic was a serious loss to the organization of poor people in Kingston.

Ten years later, I went to work as a community legal worker at a legal clinic that was the progeny of that effort, funded by the Ontario Legal Aid Plan. I was to advocate on behalf of poor people who were having problems with social assistance, employment insurance, workers' compensation, their landlord and so on. Half of my job was to be community organizing: helping the clients of the clinic empower themselves for justice. The board that hired me was made up of quite progressive people including representatives from the Union of Injured Workers and some poverty action groups. We were very effective at creating turmoil and pressuring for change.

In the six years I was there, I saw the legal establishment and the Ontario government move to strip clinics of this organizing function and increase the distance between clinic clients and clinic workers. This was accomplished in the following ways:

- The administrative requirements of the sole funding body were increased, so that hours of each board meeting and staff time were spent justifying our existence. Many of the less educated members of the board dropped off because they didn't understand the language.
- A means and assets form was introduced so that our first interaction with someone coming into the clinic was to ask them a lot of personal questions that were not directly relevant to their visit. It made an equal relationship impossible.
- Instead of clients dealing with one worker from the moment they came into the clinic they might now deal with three. They would see an intake worker or a duty counsel, and then a legal worker and then a lawyer. It was very disorienting.
- Work around rent review and repairs to slum apartments was dropped, even though the clinic had a very high success rate, and this was one of the key places to organize and teach self-help methods.

The clinic ceased to empower its clients or to help people with similar concerns get together to challenge the decision-makers; it became an advocate for individual cases that left the power structure intact. Like the Ombudsman's office, clinics are funded by government to channel the rightful anger of people who are cut off welfare, denied EI, unjustly evicted or treated unfairly by the system in other ways. Were the clinic not there, these victims might be organizing, demonstrating and generally raising hell in government offices across the nation. On the other hand, they might be sunk in poverty, horizontal violence and despair, and being recruited to a populist movement that offers law, order and conscription as solutions to their misery.

Contradiction: Packaging Community Development

The term "community development" signals the packaging of a process that ordinary people have engaged in with greater or lesser success for years. This package consists of cataloguing the skills that enable people to develop collective self-reliance by working together to plan and carry out activities, in order to facilitate the intervention of an outside agency in their lives. Once the process is packaged, it can be purchased, taught and managed. Community development becomes a component of courses in social work, agricultural extension programs and international development. It becomes a service for which consultants receive salaries. Once someone in a community or group becomes (or is introduced as) the "community development expert," everyone else starts to feel like they don't know anything about it. They devalue their own knowledge. And often the "expert" finds it is in their own self-interest to maintain this fiction.

On the other hand, there is really nothing wrong with demystifying and packaging some of these skills: they are useful tools. A community development package can be an attempt to divert the community's attention from enterprises that are likely to do enormous damage. For example, mining companies offer community development services to communities where they want to build their mines. In the Philippines, where Canadian-owned TVI intended to build a huge open pit gold mine on lands that belonged to the Subanon people, they tried to win the people over with a goat-herding project, a health clinic and a school. Most community members knew the mine was going to destroy their livelihoods and they were strongly opposed to it. Despite substantial support for the Subanon and opposition to the mine from the public and within the Canadian parliament and civil service, the government of the day — through the Canadian International Development Agency — funded the goat-herding project. Getting funds from this project and treatment from the clinic depended on support for the mine. As a result of the mine, the Subanon's villages were impoverished, and the downstream community of Siocon, which had been self-sufficient in food, found its waters poisoned by cyanide and acid drainage.

A number of large non-governmental organizations (NGOs), like World

Vision, accept huge sums of money from mining companies to undertake these sorts of programs, enabling a predatory mining company to trade on their name and reputation in order to persuade the community and the government to accept a new mine that they might otherwise reject.

Some community development packages are really designed only to get community input and volunteer time in a government program. When I was approached to work for private businesses that were bidding on contracts for public housing redesign or health promotion strategies in Sudbury, I found that most of them talked about "community development" but meant setting up a few community meetings to forestall public protest over the plan.

Sometimes the language of development is used to manipulate acceptance of new technologies and systems that tie communities into dependency on complex and expensive machinery and expertise. Under the guise of community development, the "Green Revolution" (agri-business farming technology and methods) was brought to Africa and traditional farming methods were lost.[5] Under the guise of community development, remote Indigenous communities became increasingly dependent on a wage economy and were forced to accept economic plans based on a profit model.[6]

Contradiction: The Social Economy

In recent years, "community economic development," or the "social economy," has attracted even right-wing government funding interests. It can be a variation of "pulling yourself up by your own bootstraps" — with impoverished communities being held responsible for problems created by corporate and government policies and actions.

Governments are under pressure from small towns in rural areas to maintain the population base by finding alternatives to employment in resource-based industries (mining, forestry, fishing and farming) as the resources are depleted.[7] In urban centres, under pressure from economic migrants from all over the world, governments may see community economic development as a means to deal with poverty through minimal investments.

> As inner cities have decayed as a result of capital and population flight: rural areas have been depopulated and are home to growing levels of economic distress as small farms are swallowed by larger, often corporate enterprises, and small towns atrophy; and Canada's north has become home to some particularly egregious examples of poverty and its associated indignities, the result in large part of the expansion of capitalism in search of resources.[8]

A lot of wealth is generated in all of our communities, but it does not stay there. Rather than facilitating a process to bring wealthy enterprises into the community, community economic development — as progressives frame it — focuses on local wealth creation and retention (see Chapter 11). Community economic development, as corporate interests see it, is just the opposite. It can be a way to keep local elites from screaming. Money is put into investment funds that allow people to start small businesses and to test out expansion ideas. These funds support the set up of franchises or branch plants of large companies, or the start-up of small businesses that are dependent on the computer hardware and software of large companies, or that pay out most of their income to the bank for loans and mortgages.

For example, when MiningWatch Canada approached a federal agency in northern Ontario for money to conduct community workshops on the social, environmental and economic impacts of mining, the project officer advised us that he could not recommend funding because the mining industry would be upset. On the other hand, the same agency provided millions in funding to the "Discover Abitibi" initiative, "a massive undertaking to accelerate mineral exploration and discovery in the Kirkland Lake and Timmins areas."[9]

Contradictions: Getting Money from Foundations

Getting funds from foundations requires similar skill to getting funds from government: we have to adapt our agenda to their funding requirements. Originally, large foundations like Rockefeller and Ford were set up specifically to gather information on and propose alternatives to socialist programs. All foundations serve as tax shelters for the very rich.

Canadian law and regulation is set up to make it almost impossible for NGOs and community organizations to fund advocacy work. Foundations and granting agencies depend on having "charitable status" under the income tax legislation in order to exist, and that law specifies that "charitable purposes" are, generally speaking, education, research and the relief of poverty. Foundations can only give money to charities, and in order to maintain the charitable designation, groups can only have 10 percent of their activity be "advocacy." Advocacy in Canada includes public education, lobbying for a cause and opposing or even supporting a particular law or regulation. Because of years of very sophisticated lobbying to get this rule changed, there is now some wiggle room available to groups that have the energy and where-with-all to use it.

However, the overall impact of these laws and policies is a great reluctance on the part of funders to support advocacy work and a corresponding fear on the part of incorporated community groups that they will lose their funding if they take it on.

There are, however, some foundations that are accessible to social change groups and do support innovative community work. In Canada, the Laidlaw, EJLB, Gordon, McLean, Maytree, Atkinson, Tides and McConnell foundations have quite often funded parts of our work. Canada also has a network of community foundations, which manages money for small donors. Some of this money may be directed funding, but in other cases, the network provides a good source for our work. Some unions have social justice funds, paid for by their members. Information about foundations is available from the internet, in public libraries or from the Canadian Centre for Philanthropy.

Applying effectively to a private funding source has become a sophisticated trade. Applicants need an attractively prepared presentation of their organization, audited financial statements and members who are able and willing to spend time building relationships with staff of the foundations. The group will also have to have charitable status with Revenue Canada or an agreement with a sponsor that does. Getting money from any source is about developing relationships with the people in charge and the project officer and treating them as a partner in what we are trying to do. If we do get the money, we need to be sure to write excellent reports on time.

Another consideration for accepting government and foundation funding is that it probably comes in large chunks and increases our expectations of what we will be able to accomplish. For example, we start to rely on staffing and lose our volunteer base. The mountains of paperwork required for the proposal and the reporting for the project exclude semi-literate people from positions of power within an organization. It encourages us to organize on a multiplicity of issues with separate organizations for each one, instead of trying to form a more broadly based community group where we might decide that these issues have our powerlessness in common, and we need to be more strategic in tackling them.

Contradiction: Corporate Funding

Accepting funding from corporations is a matter that requires considerable debate within an organization. What does the corporation want in return? To what extent are we condoning their behaviour towards the people and environment in other parts of Canada and other countries? Will our name be used to sell their products or give them legitimacy? Is it worth it? Frankly, I would not touch corporate funding unless it were a formal joint venture that my community controlled.

Contradiction: Gambling

In most impoverished communities, bingos are popular outings that combine a social event with the possibility of a windfall. Gambling is a significant part of Canadian culture. Our entire financial system is based on gambling: the wealthy gamble on the stock market, and the poor have lotteries.

> Under Canadian law, only the government (and its licensed agents), charities, and the horse-racing industry are legally entitled to offer

gambling to the public. Although private bets between individuals (e.g., card games, sports bets) are legal, any game in which an unlicensed third party (e.g., a bookie or the owner of a card room) makes a profit from the betting is illegal. Privately run sports books, card rooms, numbers games (lotteries), and unlicensed casinos are therefore illegal.[10]

A number of Aboriginal communities have been taking control of bingos, lotteries and casinos as sources of funds. For example, Casino Rama in Ontario negotiated with the Ontario government to set up the Casino Rama First Nations Fund, which distributes the profits to First Nations across the province. The money gambled at the casino can be spent on recreation, economic development and alcohol treatment programs. Casino Rama helped fund the Kitchenumaykoosib Inninuwug sovereignty struggle. And the casino itself may provide employment in the community. Gambling that is controlled by the community redistributes the wealth of gamblers and is certainly fairer than the class system.

However, there are two serious downsides to the gambling industry. The first is that most gambling establishments are not owned or managed by local communities, and the profits go elsewhere. The second is gambling addiction, which can lead not only to personal and family misery but to loan-sharking. Frequently, gambling venues rely upon organized crime for finance, protection, security and the collection of debts, which has obvious serious consequences for the local community.[11]

Supporting Our Own Work

We do too little to build and rely on our own resources. We are afraid to ask the people we work with to contribute financially, as we know they are already stretched. However, building a vibrant movement to transform power will require us all to put our money with our mouth is. Donor campaigns, whether direct mail, internet-based or person-to-person do not have to be big to be effective. Even a small community group can use the city directory to find names to solicit. Of course, this won't work unless people have previously heard of the group and respect it. Kim Klein's *Fundraising for Social Change* is an essential guide.[12]

Organizing concerts, bake sales, rummage sales and benefits not only raises money for day-to-day operations but has important spinoff effects in the community. Even in impoverished communities there is often money available if people feel that the activity is important enough to their own or their children's self-interest. A lot of things can be done by local people with "in kind" donations if they feel the organization is relevant to them.

Credit Unions and Alternative Investment Funds

A number of progressive organizations and individuals have set up funds that will make loans to "high risk–low return" ventures out of their regular investment portfolios. Credit unions like the Assiniboine Credit Union in Winnipeg, Bread and Roses in Toronto and Vancity in Vancouver specialize in helping community enterprises get loans. They are very willing to share their experience with others.

The Solidarity Fund in Quebec was established and maintained with deductions from the wages of workers in the major unions in Quebec. It has assisted in rescue operations of companies that were being closed by multinationals and supported a number of community economic development projects like the Project Economique du Pointe St. Charles (P.E.P). It stimulated the formation of the Québec Social Economy Trust.

> One example of the potential offered by this is the Québec Social Economy Trust. With a $22.8 million dollar initial investment from the federal government, a further $30 million in capital was leveraged from private and public sources. In its initial operations between July 2007 and September 2008, the Trust invested $6.4 million in 19 social economy enterprises, generating a total investment of $31.9 million, enabling the creation and consolidation of over 524 jobs.[13]

In Montreal, the Third Avenue Resource Centre spearheaded a project to establish a community development corporation in the impoverished Grand Plateau area of the city. They quickly discovered that they needed capital to assist small businesses to get started. In a few years they had formed an investment fund and begun to make loans at low interest to local individuals so that they could help make the Grand Plateau area more self-reliant. Capital for the fund came from the City of Montreal, churches, community groups, foundations and individual donations.

Navigating a Rough Terrain

It should be clear by now that there is no easy solution to the contradictions posed by seeking funding for social change work. Until we can establish a base of concerned people who will support the social change project with their own membership contributions and unpaid time, we will be faced with seeking money from sources that will, in turn, seek to control our work. Central to building a neighbourhood movement is developing the willingness of participants to put their own money, time and energy into it.

We can and should take foundation and government money, but we should diversify the sources and programs from which it comes. Government (like some foundations) is a site of low-intensity conflict, and we can never be sure that even the decent programs will remain that way for long. The less we rely on any individual funder, the better. Activists are always seeking ways to support one another financially, but if we do find funding to begin this kind of work, it has to be on our own agenda.

When we care about social change, we think about how we organize our own lives to be as free as possible to do real work. Real organizing for change is a way of life, not a job. We have to want to do it badly enough to find the time and money ourselves, to lobby wealthy friends, to ask for bequests from the disaffected children of the rich.

Most of the jobs we get waste our time or use it for destructive purposes: we sell our labour to earn the means of survival for ourselves and our families. Most of us have had to sell it to large corporations or the government, where what we produce will be determined by their need for profit, control or just "measurable results." People who work full-time need to think about how to use relationships with people at work, or the job itself, for the social change project. The following are a few ways people manage to do work for change.

Some activists develop lifestyles that free them from the need for full-time work. They share income, accommodation, garden produce, appliances, child-rearing, vehicles, wine-making. They get part-time work so they have more time to organize. They take turns working for money.

Young people find hundreds of places and ways to start organizing. They get groups together at school or with their friends, or they join an existing group that interests them. They organize around issues that affect them as youth: police harassment, homelessness, repressive and irrelevant schools, parents, tuition fees for colleges and universities. They form the backbone of a number of environmental, justice and peace groups.

People on social assistance or employment insurance or a pension sometimes have more time to lead organizations. In many groups from peace to playgrounds, they provide the hours of volunteer time that keep the group going. They organize with others in the same position, or with their neighbours around childcare, buyers clubs, cooperative cars, community gardens, housing, alternative medical care, imaginative schools, the Raging Grannies.

Recognizing that democratic organizations like labour unions, churches and non-profit organizations are sites of struggle, we insist that they act democratically. We fight to get and maintain access to these institutions so that they are relevant to the long-term needs of people.

We support those people within institutions like credit unions, unions, churches and governments who struggle to hold on to staff time, resources and money that can be used by the movement. It isn't any fun spending weekends in church meetings trying to ensure that money continues to go to justice work. It doesn't always feel worth it to butt one's head against a wall in the union or the service club or the office, trying to get them to free up resources for change. People who work in these places are engaged in the institutional sites of low intensity conflict. We need to support each other, sympathize, strategize and celebrate victories together.

In the long run, we need to build movements strong enough to force governments to be accountable to the public, not the corporations, so that the enormous resources we need for social change will be available for the work.

Notes

1. Although most of this information is from my own files, I have also drawn on Ian Hamilton, *The Children's Crusade* (Toronto: Peter Martin Associates, 1970); and Margaret Daly, *The Revolution Game* (New York: New Press, 1970).
2. Ian Hamilton, *The Children's Crusade*, p. 298.
3. Results-based management remains the norm in government funding to NGOs. Requirements for measurable "outputs" and "outcomes" at the beginning of projects seriously limit the ability of a project or an organizer to respond to emerging or shifting community needs and demands.
4. Roxana Ng, *The Politics of Community Services* (second edition) (Halifax: Fernwood Publishing, 1996).
5. Basil Davidson, *The Black Man's Burden: Africa and the Curse of the Nation State* (New York: Three Rivers Press, 1992).
6. Mona Etienne and Eleanor Leacock, *Women and Colonization: Anthropological Perspectives* (New York: Praeger, 1980).
7. I am grateful to Gayle Broad, Eric Shragge, John Loxley, Melanie Conn, Bibiana Seaborn, Dal Brodhead and Ted Jackson for their insights on community economic development
8. John Loxley, Jim Silver and Kathleen Sexsmith, *Doing Community Economic Development* (Halifax: Fernwood Publishing and the Canadian Centre for Policy Alternatives, 2007).
9. *Kirkland Lake Local News,* "Discover Abitibi and NEOnet Receive Cash from FedNor," March 1, 2003.
10. Peter Ferentzy and Nigel Turner, "Gambling and Organized Crime — A Review of the Literature," *Journal of Gambling Issues* 23, June, 2009, p. 111.
11. Peter Ferentzy and Nigel Turner. "Gambling and Organized Crime."
12. Kim Klein, *Fundraising for Social Change* (fifth edition) (Mississauga: John Wiley and Sons, 2007).
13. Canadian CED Network, *Pre-Budget Brief, August 2009,* <http://www.ccednet-rcdec.ca>.

Part 5

Asserting Political Power

The Donovan neighbourhood celebrates protecting The Mountain

13

Fighting for Shelter in Sudbury

In 1983, there was a terrible housing crisis in Sudbury. Inco, the major employer, had shut down for six months to try to save themselves some money during a period when the price of nickel was low. So a lot of people were out of work and losing their homes. In 1982, the interest rates had also gone way up, and this made the situation worse.

I was working in the Sudbury Community Legal Clinic. Day after day Inco workers were coming in who had lost their houses to the Canada Mortgage and Housing Corporation through power of sale and foreclosure and were looking for some place to live. Their vacant houses would sit there empty while they were homeless. At the same time, landlords were finding excuses to evict single parent mums and kids to rent to "more desirable tenants" — an Inco worker with a family.

The Sudbury Housing Authority, also wanting these "desirables," began to do what they called "preventive maintenance checks." They would go into the home of a woman who had been living there for sixteen years and find every little thing that was wrong with the house — a lot of which was due to Sudbury Housing's neglect — and say if she didn't pay $2000 damages, she would be evicted. So the impact of the layoffs from the company was extending to single parent women and kids.

A group of us had been working over the years around housing, and we started to talk about what we could do. Some of us began to call ourselves United Tenants. UT was mostly comprised of single parent women I had met through my work when they had organized their building or confronted their slum landlord. We were joined by a few staff people from the Neighbourhood Action Project (NAP), and we decided to do whatever we could to get more affordable housing, to prevent evictions and so on. We met in NAP's tiny office, where there weren't enough chairs, and we'd talk about things and laugh with each other and plan.

At the same time, the regional government had got together an ad hoc group of people called the HELP committee, comprised of human services managers, church leaders, a representative from Inco and Falconbridge (the mining companies) and a representative from the Steelworkers Union.

They were expected to find ways of dealing with the crisis. I was able to get appointed to the group after the union representative lobbied on my behalf to the regional chair of Sudbury.

Although a lot of the committee activities were "window-dressing," some people on it were really concerned. This smaller group used the HELP committee to establish a phone-in radio show to give information about welfare, landlord problems, foreclosures and so on. One morning a man called in; he and his family had been living with his parents for a month. They were all going crazy because the place was so small, and he thought it was going to get violent because everyone was so angry at each other.

With me on the show that day was the public relations officer from Inco, Ernie Hedigan, and Ernie St. Jean from the Steelworkers Local 6500. Hedigan simply couldn't believe that this family was unable to find housing. St. Jean and I told him about how serious the housing crisis had become even while there were 120 houses sitting vacant that belonged to CMHC, a crown corporation. "Why can't we get those houses rented to the homeless?" we asked. And he said, "Well, of course we can. We'll just go to the Canada Mortgage and Housing Corporation and say, rent them."

So a little delegation from the group went to CMHC and asked. Well, they couldn't do it because the policy said the houses had to be sold, not rented. The man from Inco simply couldn't believe it. He was very upset because it was his company's shutdown that was creating the problem, and he was the public relations officer, and here was this government organization that wouldn't do what he wanted. I laughed and said, "Maybe if we sat in at Inco, CMHC would be made to move." He looked embarrassed.

Practically every time someone new was going to be homeless, I would find out at the legal clinic because the victim would come to us for help to fight the eviction or to get welfare, or to get a hydro deposit and whatever. Day after day, they came.

I made it my job to involve the HELP Committee members in looking for housing for each and every one of these families. Soon there was no doubt in any of their minds of the severity of the crisis. For the first time in their lives they realized how terrible it was not to have much money, to have children and no place to live. Most of them had never had this experience. They always thought that if you wanted something bad enough you could somehow get it.

They wrote letters and presented briefs to the provincial and federal governments. They pressured the regional government. At one point we even held a meeting of all the levels of government that were involved in housing to try and get an agreement worked out. Nothing happened.

United Tenants realized they had to do something to increase the pressure. That summer Tom Rummel and his wife and two kids had no place to live. The Rummels were the kind of family that the whole community could sympathize with: a laid-off miner, a hard worker, a good marriage, cute children, the whole bit. As usual, the HELP committee tried to persuade CMHC to rent them a home. Then we begged the regional government for emergency housing. When this got nowhere, United Tenants helped the family put up a tent at Memorial Park in downtown Sudbury.

UT sent out press releases and press packets. We arranged with the mayor to keep the pressure on CMHC and the province, if he'd keep the police off the family. We even arranged for round-the-clock support, food and tents. We organized clowns and music and theatre. It took two days before the Rummels were housed, and it was a private citizen who offered them a place. Even though we kept sending deputations to CMHC, they still wouldn't budge.

Then in August, another friend of ours, a single parent, had no place to go. Every day, she walked past a house owned by CMHC that was for sale on Melvin Street. "I want that house," Paulette said. So once again the HELP committee started going to CMHC and asking for it. We intimated to them that she was angry enough to just move in if they didn't agree. Within a day, CMHC suddenly had a vacancy in a regular rental unit in Apollo Terrace. I still don't know how they found it. She moved in.

Of course, a few weeks later there was another family with no place to go. There were always lots of families in this position, but most of them were too afraid to fight back. This family was ready. UT had a meeting with the family, and they wanted to move into the Melvin Street house. "That house is sitting there empty. These people need a place to live. Which is the more important right, private property or shelter?"

It was agreed that unless the Landrys were housed within a week, we would occupy the house. We sent a delegation to tell the HELP committee of our decision. Because the HELP committee membership were people with "clout," with titles and positions, we felt we needed them to give strength to our situation. By now they were just as frustrated and angry as anybody else, and they agreed that we should go ahead. The HELP committee sent a delegation to the regional chair and said that unless the family was housed in twenty-four hours, they could not be responsible for what might happen. The regional chair sent a telegram to the premier of the province and to CMHC asking them to intervene. Like us, he hoped that the pressure tactic would free up money or policies to help the crisis. But nothing happened.

So the day the Landry family moved into 370 Melvin Street, there were a hundred people, including representatives of the bishop and the head of the Ministers Association, to help them. (The Inco guy said that although he supported us, he'd better not be seen there). The MPP, Floyd Laughren, was the first to cross the threshold. There were twenty women with their kids from United Tenants, and they moved into the house. Because we had warned the press, they were all there too. Hydro and heat were on in the house, but there was no water. After a phone conversation with the union representing regional workers, they drove up and turned the water on.

The Landrys and their supporters stayed in the house for a week. We couldn't ever leave them alone, because we didn't know when the police were going to come to evict us. We had wonderful press; they loved it.

The time in the house was exhausting. No one got enough sleep. You had to worry about how you would feed all these people, women worried about the Children's Aid Society taking their kids. Also, the house became a centre for helping others. A woman would come in and say "My refrigerator isn't working," and people would go off and fix it. It was an exciting time. It became a place where, when things needed to be done, you did 'em. When CMHC officials went through on inspections, we would all gather in the living room and sing.

Meanwhile, the negotiations with CMHC and the province appeared to be going nowhere. We were all getting quite nervous. Then our lawyer called and said that the Crown had decided on charges. We had all thought they would only charge us with mischief as a summary offence. But they had decided to charge us with mischief as an indictable offence, which can carry up to fourteen years in prison. The squatters had a meeting right away to talk about it. Mrs. Landry was too exhausted to continue; her husband wanted to be a hero and go to jail. The group felt that they didn't have the energy to sustain a legal defence over a long period of time. We debated whether to move the pressure to the Inco offices or the region. Finally, we came to an agreement to move the demonstration to the regional government offices the next day.

The next morning we cleaned the house and then marched to the regional offices. We sat in the big foyer there and sang songs, while members of the HELP committee negotiated with the regional chair about his responsibility to find this family emergency shelter. Later that day, one of the city workers succeeded in talking a slumlord into renting them a place. Within four months the Landrys got public housing.

It is almost impossible to believe that it took so much effort just to get one family a home. But the struggle gained much more than that one home. It built the credibility and power of UT, which continued to advocate on housing issues. Within a few months, the region established an emergency housing agreement, so that people like the Rummels and the Landrys could move in to vacant CMHC houses. And that year, Sudbury received far more than its share of non-profit and cooperative housing money. We were able to make our new non-profits 85 percent rent-geared-to-income instead of the usual 45 percent. Funding was also received for a crisis housing organization, which continued advocacy on the issues.

Our work made a substantial improvement in the lives of the most desperate in the community. The people who were involved in the battle built relationships with one another, and many became life-long community leaders and activists.

14

Organizing Campaigns

Most community-based groups never plan political campaigns; they lurch from issue to issue and event to event, without focusing their attention on a campaign to get political changes. The term "campaign" is a military one and is sometimes rejected by organizers because they feel it treats the world like a battleground and allows us to objectify the "enemy."

However, I see "campaign" as a useful term. When we work for change we take on an entrenched way of doing things that benefits some people enough that they will probably try to stop us from making the change. If we focus our organizing energy on the change we want to see and figure out the steps we need to take to make it a reality, we can be much more effective.

The problem with most campaign organizing is that it rarely gets at the systemic relationships of power. It seeks to influence decision-makers, not to change the structures in which they operate. When we want to force a power structure, like government, to listen to us and make changes we want or need, the campaign works roughly like that experienced with the Sudbury housing crisis. As a group, we are concerned or outraged by something. We come together around the concern, research the issue and then embark on actions to push for the change we want. The first action is likely to be more educational than confrontational (a petition, a protest, a public meeting). We may or may not have a plan beyond the first action, but the need for a strategy will escalate as we go along. Usually we start by going through all the "proper channels." At this point, if we have the support of some known community leaders, we will be able to engage a lot of the public and the press on our side. If not, we will have to re-track and build the base. When (and if) the proper channels are blocked, we can up the pressure on the decision-makers.

It helps to have an "inside strategy," that is, to identify and work with some public servants who will champion our cause within government or the corporation. Remember, the values people hold in their hearts are often different than what they do for a living, and they may be looking for some way to keep their self-respect by taking a few chances. Some of these allies will reveal themselves to us as we go along; others will be found through the hard work of lobbying. They may be running serious risks to their employment by supporting us, and so we should treat the relationship with discretion and respect.

As we go along, we will begin to be a "credible threat," and we will have opportunity to start negotiating with people who hold power. We will have to prove we are not bluffing. We may need to create a dramatic action to show them the high level of public support for the issue. We will probably be faced with lots of detail work to sustain the campaign itself.

Then the cycle begins again. There will be stonewalling and delays by some bureaucrats; they may try taking care of the individual and not the root problem. There will be attempts to evade responsibility. We will make all this known to our supporters and organize a bigger action.

When it gets to this stage, major corporate powerholders will begin moving behind the scenes to find a solution to the conflict; they will increase their lobbying with government. We may get some concessions, and moves will be made to disorganize us. If we can hold on, then the decision-makers might find a way to meet our full demands without appearing to give in to us. If we can't weather the storm, our group disintegrates.

In the last analysis, all organizing efforts mean that we are going to confront a "power structure" — those people who are benefiting from the way things are now and who control dollars, resources and labour that could solve the problem.[1] But first off, we have to come to terms with who "we" — ourselves and our group — are.

Who Is "We"?

Elizabeth May writes:

> The thought runs through our mind: "someone ought to do something." It may not occur to you immediately that that someone is you! My first essential piece of advice is to skip the initial stage of hand-wringing frustration. Do not waste time lamenting that there is nothing you can do. Get busy! Find out who else in our circle of friends or larger community is also outraged. Meet for a coffee. Send out an e-mail.[2]

Elizabeth is right, but the strategies and actions open to us as social activists depend on who I and my group are: where we are located in the world. The work will force us to ask these questions over and over again as we go forward. Where we are lacking, we will need to organize to involve others who bring a different perspective to the work.

So, for example, if I am a white, female senior, in order to create a broad-based movement I will have to consciously think about identifying and encouraging leadership that is racialized, possibly male and/or young. If I am paid to work on this issue, I may have a very different stake in it than someone who is involved because they are victimized by it. If I live in the wilderness but have high-speed internet I will organize differently than someone with no internet access at all.

What Do We Want to Change: Choosing the Goal

We work with an issue or situation for which our group feels real passion, preferably one where we have first-hand knowledge and that affects us personally. Any situation exists in a web of relationships and is part of a history. Just by choosing this focus, we are making a statement. Sometimes the issue or situation chooses us.

We ask ourselves what we really want? What would the ideal situation look like? What would have to happen to achieve the ideal situation? Is there a reason why we should not ask for the ideal solution? What would happen if we did? The possibilities and boundaries will expand and contract throughout a struggle.

For example, I may feel that every tenant in this city is getting ripped off and should have the right to shelter; that everyone is entitled to enough space and comfort to live decently; and that a person's income should have nothing to do with accessibility to housing. To take action, my group needs to decide on a way to focus this dream. It may be presented to us in the form of a single issue: some people with no place to live, no emergency shelter, an unconscionable rent increase in an apartment building, a slum landlord who doesn't do repairs, a series of illegal evictions. We can take on a single issue and still tell the truth about what we really want. The bigger dream weaves the individual issues together.

This means that my community and I have to struggle with all these problems if we want a realistic strategy. We can say what we really want and make that known. We can begin to rebuild the fabric of the community. And then we have to figure out a strategy to protect what we already have and to get as much self-determination as possible without jeopardizing our ability to make more demands later when we are stronger as a community.

Too often we limit our demands to what the power structures allow us to have — to "winnable" requests. This is a frustrating and pointless exercise. We do not know what we can win until we try. Elizabeth May says: "We have to do what we have to do, Miracles happen. The life force of the planet is very strong. Dandelions poke through sidewalks. We don't know enough to give up. We only know enough to know we have to change the course of human events."[3]

Neighbourhood Organizing

Saul Alinsky, the author of *Reveille for Radicals*,[4] was a famous American community organizer. Starting with the Back of the Yards, a working-class neighbourhood in Chicago, Alinsky developed a style of organizing that was very similar to the trade union organizing of John L. Lewis (his hero and friend). Back of the Yards and other Alinsky organizing drives all began with a crisis in a community. The leaders of formal community institutions (mostly churches) would get together and ask the organizer to "come into the community." They would also commit to raising the money for the organizing.

The organizer hired a staff and they spent their time talking with community-based groups and going door-to-door in the neighbourhood challenging and encouraging people to get involved in the community organization. The organizers helped the people select a "winnable" issue first, and then the people (now "the organization") confronted the politicians or corporate official whom they identified as having the power to change the situation. The same strategy was used again and again, building the confidence and leadership abilities of the local people who got involved.

One of the most famous neighbourhood organizing projects in Canada was Riverdale Community Organization in Toronto's East End in the mid-1970s and early 1980s. Don Keating, who was the original organizer on the project, wrote a book about it called *The Power to Make It Happen*.[5] The following are key assumptions of neighbourhood organizing:

- The underlying problem of the neighbourhood is one of powerlessness, and the twin goals are to win results and build power.
- People respond best when given an opportunity to choose their own issues.
- "Those who fix problems are the ones who increase their strength. We must not give our issues away for someone else to solve.... We do our own fixing by dealing with the person causing or responsible for the problem.... Deal directly with our adversaries."
- "To build strong organization, the people with the problems need to be involved in winning the results.... Choose a method that can best be expected to produce results on the problems and involve the greatest number of people affected."
- "There are limits to the amount of pressure any power-holder can withstand even from a group of 'nobodies' and no one is invulnerable."[6]

Neighbourhood organizing delivered results. A lot of "nobodies" got a taste of leading a group and people learned that sticking together could win some issues for their neighbourhood and how ineffectual and scared a lot of public leaders really were. It made immediate and concrete improvements in the lives of people in poor neighbourhoods. There is no substitute for the hard work of going door-to-door, organizing household by household. This kind of community empowerment works, but it is labour intensive, and it rarely — in Canada — attracts funding from government or foundations.

Researching the Issue

It is crucial that we know everything we can about our issue. We have to read reliable sources and get our facts straight. If we can't understand the material, we need to find someone who does, perhaps at a university or community college. We need to call or email people whose names crop up in the literature. We need to find people who can help us understand the legal and regulatory context. We need to find out what "for the other side" says about the issue and ask them questions. We need to keep notes of key points. However, it is important not to exaggerate our position or knowledge. And it is vital to make sure that our group shares this knowledge with each other (listserves are an excellent way to do this). Throughout the campaign, there will be an on-going need for more research and information, about the issue itself, about the power structure that needs to be moved and about our allies. We ignore this need for continuing research at our peril.

Power-Mapping

Researching what would make the key players change their mind is called "power mapping." Even the most formidable power structure is only possible because of the human beings who work in it. How do we entice them to our side? We have to understand the institutions and players we need to change. Who do we want to make do what? Why aren't they doing it already? The answer to these two questions might be simple, like "so far they haven't had to" or "maybe they don't know what hardship the present situation is causing." It is a good idea to see if this is the reason before we do anything else. We can document the need and bring it to the attention of the person or people who need to make the changes. Even if they don't do anything, we will know their response, and we will have put them on notice that we are concerned about this situation.

Government is usually acting for interests other than the average voter's. Most new construction projects, like roads and buildings, are not about building hospitals closer to home or increasing jobs in an area or anything like that. They are about providing contracts to construction companies. Most changes in deficit financing are about helping banks. Most hydro projects are about helping industrial consumers, providing contracts to construction and electrical companies, and paying interest and dividends to financiers.

Who has the power to make the change we need? Who do we have to persuade? Who do the decision-makers listen to? What are they afraid of? What do their close contacts, workers, other committee members, family, think about this issue? Is there any chance to bring those close to the power-holders on-side and have them work on the people whose minds we have to change? If we are talking about a Cabinet minister or a senior bureaucrat, where are the contradictions within their own departments? Where is there space to manoeuver?

There is a difference between the power people have because of the job they do and the power they have because of their personal wealth, connections, etc. If we can't get the person with the title to move, what about finding people with personal power to influence them? We may simply be unable to get this kind of information about the people we have to change. We have to assume that they will respond to strong expressions of public opinion in support of our cause and manage our organizing efforts accordingly.

Planning Strategy

There are two things we will want to accomplish with our strategy. One may be solving the particular immediate problem of an individual: getting a house, getting a job, etc. Since it is true that the squeaky wheel gets the grease, the system will usually respond to individual cases if enough noise is made. It is more difficult if we want to make systemic change — to go after the root causes of the problem. However, even going after a root cause usually requires a "human face" or a "poster child" — the specific example that represents the larger picture.

Once we know what our goal is and have done some research to understand the issue and its context, we can start to plan strategy to get what we want. This is often best done in a workshop setting, so everyone can contribute to the ideas and map out the plan together. No matter how fancy a strategy is, if it doesn't excite the group, forget it. A good strategy is one that makes us all go, yeah! and has all of us enthusiastic and thinking about it day and night and wanting to *go*. We play around with different ideas till we find some that fit. We brainstorm, discuss, use power-mapping, try out different games. We try using the questions below.

Who else is working on this issue in our community? How will we build public interest in our cause? What rules, what laws, what systems are in the way? How do we change them and in what order? What makes those with power to make the change tick? Why are they in our way? Do they really disagree, or are they trapped too? What would unstick them? (for example, do they have kids in the movement at home?) If they really disagree, is there a way around them? Can they be removed from the way? How much people power do we need to persuade those with institutionalized power to change their minds? How will we build it?

Most bureaucracies operate smoothly as long as nothing disrupts their usual functioning. For the people who work in these places, any hot political issue means that phones ring and people need to be pacified and things have to be explained to superiors. Then they panic, because they don't have time or systems to deal with the disruption. Sometimes they will give in to us just because it will take less time and hassle to give in than to fight. Even children know this strategy sometimes works with grownups!

We think about all the things we would like to do to solve the problem and make sure to separate strategic ideas from tactics. We use buzz groups and brainstorming, and then pick those things that everyone feels the most excited about. Do we have the energy to do it? Who will do it? When? How will they be accountable to the larger group? If the group isn't excited enough to take things on, we need to scale down the plan. Do we need more people? Who would be excited by this idea and work with us? Who is going to contact them? How?

Building the Group during a Campaign

In the long run, our ability to create systemic change — to really change the power structure — is dependent on having a "mass base": a movement of large numbers of organized people who understand the power structure and are willing to take risks to change it.

Our only power for real change is in our numbers, passion and commitment. Building trust and learning to work together have to be important parts of any strategy. We need to nurture the group itself. Who is going to be responsible for growing the group, for keeping the group informed? Who talks with whom? How can we expand these networks? What will inspire others? What isn't being said? Are people really tired? Are we excited? We need to take time to celebrate our victories and our hard work and to have some fun or to reflect together.

We need to think about cultural and class differences in the group. What kind of things do we know how to do now? What skills does each person bring to the group? How can we use those skills in developing the strategy? What new skills do people want to learn? How? How do we provide honest feedback if people aren't doing something well enough? How do we provide apprenticeships?

In deciding strategy, we can work these questions through in the larger group with discussion and small groups. We can try role playing the other players in the community and seeing where there may be conflict or compromise. We can spend time making wall-sized charts of where we are in our strategy and what remains to be done. It'll make us feel well organized and terrific.

Showing Our Strength

The first part of the strategy will be invisible to the decision-makers we want to influence. We build a core group; we research the issue; we identify supporters and begin to educate the public about the issue; we plan a strategy; we figure out who can make the decision we desire. The next step usually involves presenting a brief or petition to the decision-makers asking for the changes we want. This will likely be ignored — they will promise to "study" the matter. We might then have people send letters and visit their local politicians or something similar; we will look for friendly insiders.

At a certain point, we will want to show the decision-maker that a lot of people agree with our position and offer them an opportunity to "review the situation." We can imply that we have the power to embarrass them publicly if they do not shift. The threat of an action is often more powerful than the action itself. However, an experienced power structure will know that the press will cover an action only for a short time period, and that there might be ways to disorganize our group. Also, if this is the first time we have tangled with each other, they may call our bluff, assuming we cannot pull off a very good action anyway.

We should never threaten to carry out an action unless we can carry it off, and we should never exaggerate our strength. One of the biggest mistakes inexperienced organizers make is to call demonstrations, rallies and marches to which very small numbers of people show up. Unless we know we can mobilize hundreds, we should take actions that are effective with smaller numbers, like "family" picnics, street/guerrilla theatre, information pickets or booths in shopping malls. By the way, people don't come to these kinds of events on the strength of a leaflet, an email or a newspaper story. They come because they have been organized, by us, or through their union, or through another community group.

The demonstration or other action should have a clear focus. It needs to clearly identify what we want to happen. If we name the person we want to make the decision, we may find that they entrench more deeply, so it is better not to do this. Politicians and the power structure never want to be seen to back down under pressure. We should always offer them an out.

Any demonstration has to be carefully planned. We should check to see if we need permits; or if we are going to do it without one; make sure we can get enough people to it; arrange for toilet access and for wheelchairs. What are the slogans going to be? Do we need marshals? How will people get there?

Shifting Power: The Escalating Dance

If the first action does not achieve our goal (and it rarely will), then we will be engaged in an escalating pattern of pressure on the power structure. The usual pattern is as follows:

1. We ask for support with letters, briefs, delegations, etc. through the "proper channels."
2. The organization or people we approached evade the issue in some way: "not our responsibility," "the policy says…," "not enough money," etc.
3. We make a public statement of our organization's position and begin to build support from key people, community leaders, the workers in the bureaucracy we are trying to move, unions, etc.
4. The target group/person either stonewalls, denies there is a problem, ridicules the group making the demands, or claims to be "looking into it" (giving us the run-around).
5. We continue to work through proper channels: encouraging insiders, presenting briefs, attending meetings and so on. If continued for long, the run-around can kill enthusiasm and energy in a group: it excludes people without formal education and elevates the articulate. The others will vote with their feet. On the other hand, if we are charged with "not following proper channels," we will have a difficult time getting public support. To get around this problem, we can have a small group follow the proper channels but build our pressure on the streets. For one thing, writing and presenting briefs are usually activities available only to people with middle-class skills. At the root of the problem, however, is power, and that is built with numbers and commitment. Once the formally educated people take over, working people get squeezed out, and with them, their kinds of survival knowledge and expertise. People with middle-class skills are more likely to believe that the system can be made to work through persuasion and reason. This is precisely why working people must be involved: they are less likely to think that the system can work for them. In fact, the main reason things change is because those in charge are afraid of losing their position. Often when it appears that a victory is the result of reasoned argument, in the background there is a group of angry teenagers or workers raising hell. The old tactic "If you don't talk to me, you'll have to deal with the militants" works.
6. The power structure continues to drag things out.
7. We call an action, like a demonstration or a picket, to draw public attention to the issue and to work together on an activity.
8. The decision-makers will claim publicly that they are working on the problem, and they may begin to respond with token concessions.

Alternatively, they might continue to stonewall and discredit the group. At this point, we may want to look again for openings with people within the decision-makers' structures, to try and disorganize them from within.

9. We call for a more dramatic action: an occupation, a blockade, a boycott of a major store. We build a coalition, or hook up with an existing movement, to support our demands and act together. We shift the focus of our action to the corporate mover behind the scenes (the construction company that profits from the logging road instead of the Ministry of Natural Resources; the big local developer instead of the rent review board, the major department store instead of the welfare office).

10. They try to intimidate us, with experts, cutting grants, attacks in the paper, on television, etc. They may also offer us grants to shift the direction of our organization. They may try any of the tactics discussed below.

When the Power Structure Takes Us Seriously

If our organization survives the onslaught described above, and we either continue the action or escalate it, then some people within the power structure will begin to be nervous that the structure itself is in jeopardy (and it is!). There may be a number of workers in their organization that support our position and are beginning to make noises through their union or sabotage equipment or leak important information to the press. Or perhaps the decision-makers are nervous about what elected officials will do or maybe their primacy is being attacked from inside the power structure itself.

When the contradictions and competing interests within the power structure begin to make themselves felt, one of two things can happen: There is a shift of responsibility within the structure and our demands are met (they will say that it is the previous group's fault that the matter was not addressed). Or the competing parts of the structure will unite to disorganize our group. If this happens, this is a crucial time in long-term political organizing. The power structure will respond with whatever means it feels are necessary to maintain itself. This may include illegal actions on their part and violence against us. The level of their attack is an indication of their perception of the strength of our campaign. If our movement is not strong enough at this point, we will face defeat. This is likely to contribute to fear, cynicism and despair, not to further struggle.

As the power structure responds in any of the ways described below, we need to evaluate whether we have built enough broad-based solidarity to be able to continue. Sometimes it is better to settle and keep the strength and enthusiasm we have built for another battle.

The power structure might decide to postpone things by calling a study or an environmental assessment or hiring an independent consultant to research and report on the matter. Although this may offer them an out later, it will also effectively remove the action from our turf. It will once again require the skills of formally educated people; we will have almost no choice but to participate in this study. We will need to find a way to keep our membership actively involved and to keep the issue before the public; perhaps by organizing our own public forums or bringing our people in droves to theirs.

They will probably start to use rhetoric that sounds like ours. We will have to translate what they are really saying to the public. It will require our best public relations work. Following pressure from Indigenous groups, the government now talks about "self-government"; following pressure from women's groups, the government talks about "affirmative action."

They will give us tokens, designed to split our group. They will find housing only for group leaders; they'll introduce a food program in one school; they'll make the trouble-maker at work a supervisor; they'll grant compensation to a couple of workers. It may be impossible to ask the leaders to turn down the token offer; they will get caught between loyalty to their families and loyalty to the group.

The decision-makers may claim that although they support us, they do not have the power to grant what we ask: insufficient money, not their responsibility, etc. Our response should be: if this is true, then they should work actively with our group to influence the body that has the power, and we will continue to fight for their active support of the cause. They may claim that the only way to grant what we ask is to punish some other group: they can only grant welfare reform if they tax homeowners more; they can only protect our community from nuclear waste if it goes to some other community. We have to make it clear that this is unacceptable and be ready with alternatives.

They may try to draw us into action in another forum, like the courts. This may be a strategy we have chosen for ourselves or it might be thrust upon us. We need to be very careful to evaluate the costs in money and time before we get into this position. It might be better to get out while the going is good.

We know that we have really hit a vulnerable spot in the power structure when they move to disorganize our group. Suddenly there may be people who cause trouble in meetings, or who want the group to use violent tactics, or who attack leaders who are the backbone of the group. Some of this could be a result of poor organizing on the group's part, but it could be infiltrators. There certainly is enough history of this in Canada. Whatever their motives, if the group cannot handle these people, get them out of the group and fast.

As our issue escalates and is taken up outside our community, there may be acts of violence against members of the group: threats, beatings, destruction of property, intimidation, arrests on unrelated charges, even "car accidents" and other very serious stuff. For women and children in the group, this may take the form of domestic violence or sexual harassment. If our group has been built strongly enough, then these acts may serve to bring people tighter together and build public support for the fundamental social changes we all need.

As the corporate agenda for Canada increases the gap between rich and poor and the struggle over resources and the future of this country heats up, both personal and state violence will become more prevalent. Our best protection against violence is to build a strong non-violent movement of solidarity that can speak truth and truly support one another. Using violence only begets more, and we cannot create the world we want on those terms.

Political Organizing to Affect an Institution

Organizing within the major institutions of our society is not very different than within any community. They are all sites of low intensity struggle over differing values. Public servants are workers and live very different lives at home and at work. Good organizing engages workers as people with a conscience and a desire to make a difference in the world. Within workplaces, churches, unions and non-profit organizations, we need to take our organizing very seriously. The first step in organizing in these places, as anywhere else, is to identify allies within the organization.

The following are a few basic things to remember when we are organizing to influence a bureaucracy or institution:

- Even though particular public servants may want to help us, they may have no influence in the areas where the changes need to take place. It is important to try to find someone with a real connection to the issues you are pursuing.
- Knowing the various pieces of the pie that have to be changed to get our demands met means that we can target each individually, or as important, avoid being nasty to someone who is really trying to help. For example, let's suppose that one member of our welfare rights group has been cut off. We need to know whether she has been cut off by family benefits or municipal welfare and for what reason. There will be a big difference in our tactics if the cut off is contrary to the regulations and law, or within them. If it is contrary to the regulations, we try to get current policy enforced. If it is within the law, then we try to either get an exception to a policy or get the law changed. Changing the law requires moving the government at the provincial level.
- All frontline workers have supervisors who have more power than they do to make changes and exceptions. These supervisors also report to others who have more power and so on. As we go up the line, the employees

have progressively more power and less local involvement. They are also more likely to identify their interests with the interests of the institution itself. That is how they got to the power position they hold.

- If a buck can be passed to someone else, it will be. All workers are overworked and busy. They do not want to deal with difficult tasks or problems that will take any time. Any tactic that disrupts the working day of a worker is seen with dread. Often a bureaucrat will decide to give in to pressure rather than have to waste time fighting it. All workers fear having to explain themselves to a supervisor, and supervisors dread having to explain themselves to the public. If we have effectively messed up the life of a department once or twice, then even the threat of causing this kind of disruption again can get results.

- Unionization at work means that employees are less likely to be fired for speaking their minds. Unionized workers take more chances. They also may have a forum for discussing the product of their work and the character of their workplace. We can't count on this however. Most unions provide their members with little room for discussion and are very under-serviced. Some unions are downright repressive.

- We need to remember that workers have a life outside the workplace, which is often very different from their job. The values they are forced to live at work may be in conflict with their personal values: ecologists in the Ministry of Natural Resources, for example. People deal with these conflicts in a variety of ways in order to maintain their self-respect: they become cynical; they blame the victim; they adopt corporate values; they look for ways to "get the system."

Notes

1. Four excellent resources on political strategy, which have influenced this chapter are Greg Speeter, *Power: A Repossession Manual* (Boston: University of Massachusetts, 1978); Si Kahn, *How People Get Power* (Toronto: McGraw-Hill, 1970); Bill Moyer, 2002. *Doing Democracy: The MAP Model for Organizing Social Movements* (Gabriola Island, BC: New Society Publishers, 2002); Elizabeth May, *How to Save the Planet in Our Spare Time* (Toronto: Key Porter, 2006).

2. Elizabeth May, *How to Save the Planet*, p. 17.

3. Elizabeth May, *How to Save the Planet*, p. 34.

4. Saul D. Alinsky, *Reveille for Radicals* (New York: Vintage Books, 1969).

5. Donald Keating, *The Power to Make It Happen* (Toronto: Greentree Press, 1972). The organization won over 200 issues in four years

6. Donald R. Keating, "The Future of Neighbourhood Organizing," in Dan A. Chekki, *Participatory Democracy in Action* (New Delhi: Vikas Publishing House, 1979) p. 228–31.

15

Tactics and Direct Action

Strategy and tactics are not the same things. Strategy is the long-term plan to reach our goal. Tactics are tools we use to get there. In choosing tools, we cannot forget to think holistically, to work with ideas that come from the culture, economy, relationship-building part of the medicine wheel, as well as political tools like demonstrations. We can make our demonstrations festivals of art and drama. We can work on community economic development alternatives while we disrupt the banks. We can begin our protest with a circle of prayers. We can hold a potluck supper and sleepover on the steps of city hall. We can create murals about our dreams. Most tactics are discussed elsewhere in the book: in the sections on culture, working together and economics.

In choosing tactics, it is extremely important to remember *what* we want to achieve. Generally, we want to win lots of people over to our way of thinking. We want to expose the hypocrisy and lies of the power structures in a way that enables people to hear us. We want to encourage the people working within institutions of power to join us and agree with us. And we want people to believe that "another world is possible." Tactics that people perceive as hostile or crazy will only alienate them. Remember, people are afraid, and frightened people protect themselves and their families first; they don't join social change organizations.

Sometimes, however, direct action — the assertion of our responsibility to protect the earth and one another — is necessary. People act to protect endangered spaces and resist destruction of land, water and community.

Diversity of Tactics

There is an on-going debate in the global justice movement about "diversity of tactics," particularly about the relationship of the majority non-violent protestors to the "black bloc" or other groups that advocate destruction of property as a tactic in the larger struggle. In large demonstrations, it is impossible to control the actions of all the participants without creating our own enforcement — such as demonstration marshals. In Canada there is little public support for destructive tactics, and the media focus on the most aggressive of the protestors. Property destruction tends to alienate the larger public, interferes with our claims to the "moral high ground" and leaves us open to infiltrators — "agents provocateurs." In general, there are always undercover police in the most aggressive groups — often advocating the most dramatic actions.

There is an enormous difference between destruction of property — especially the property owned and controlled by global corporations — and intentionally injuring humans, a privilege reserved in Canada to the state. However, the choice of destruction of property or other violence as a weapon will also escalate violence from the state and the corporate world, where we are completely out-classed and cannot win. It is like enraging an elephant with a BB gun.

On the other hand, in Europe and most other parts of the world, destruction of property is an accepted part of demonstrations — rioting, burning cars and throwing cobblestones are expected parts of any demonstration. It is hard not to sympathize with the rage that drives people who undertake these actions. Many of them experience violence against their person on a daily basis.

Starhawk writes: "But non-violence is not about avoiding violence; rather, it is the refusal to inflict violence…. The essence of passive resistance is the refusal to obey unjust laws, the willingness to act and to risk, to disrupt business as usual, not through violence but through non-compliance. Pacifism also does not imply an unwillingness to defend oneself or one's family from a violent attack. Pacifism is the refusal to use violence for political ends."[1]

To me, non-violence is a moral stand as well as a strategic one in the Canadian context. We have to live the change we want to create in the world

Boycotts

Boycotts mean organizing people to refuse to deal with a store, individual or government that we want to persuade. A sustained boycott is labour intensive and can be very effective. We are probably most familiar with national and international boycotts against the following: Shell Oil, Nestle, Kraft, California grapes, Victoria's Secret.

Community groups use boycotts for different reasons:

- To get one part of the power structure to pressure another part: boycotting a local stationary store over an education cutback, so that the owner will pressure his friends on the board of education to change their minds.
- To end a discriminatory practice at one institution: for example, boycot-

ting a bar where women staff have been sexually harassed or where they have refused to hire Indigenous people.

- To indicate public outrage at the behaviour of a public body: boycotting hearings, elections and administrative tribunals. This kind of boycott is usually of short duration.
- To force a merchant or other organization to change their behaviour: for example, refusing to shop at stores that will not give credit to strikers or refusing to shop in stores that sell war toys.
- To be in solidarity with a national or international boycott.

In undertaking a boycott, we need to be clear about *who* we want to have do *what*. We need to be careful not to overestimate the willingness of the public to support the boycott. It is easy to have a boycott backfire and actually increase the business of a merchant or give extra air-time to our opponents. A boycott can go on for a very long time, so often it is wise to determine a way to end it if we need to and not lose face.

We need to make sure we really have something significant to withdraw from the target — and that they will regret losing our support. When our women's group decided to withdraw all its money from the Toronto-Dominion Bank because of its investments in South Africa, we had a demonstration at the branch as we took the money out. We sent the signing officers into the bank to get the money, only to watch as they had to pay off the overdraft to close the account. Not a disaster but certainly embarrassing. The bank was not sorry to see us go.

Blockades and Occupations

Blockades are becoming one of the most effective and popular tools of the Aboriginal struggle and of the environmental movement. Workers and/or community people can choose to disrupt or take over the functioning of a company or a government institution from the inside, as workers have done in Argentina and other countries.

Blockades and occupations are usually illegal, and charges can range from a summary offence of mischief or trespass to heavier indictable offences. There is also the possibility that the organization will be sued for damages that we have caused, including loss of income to the target group and policing costs. The Kitchenuhmaykoosib Inninnuwug First Nation was sued for $10 billion for blockading the mining exploration company Platinex in northern Ontario. Despite this, the movement they built in support of their cause enabled them to protect their land, and the suit was later dropped. Because this kind of civil disobedience is so dramatic, it is a very effective way of resisting. Blockades and occupations are a good tactic when:

- we have a reason of sufficient seriousness that a good part of the public will support civil disobedience;
- we have a large and committed enough membership to sustain the blockade, occupation or work-in. They can last a few days or years;
- we have the "moral high-ground" on the issue, for example, asserting jurisdiction;
- we are clear about whether we intend the action to actually stop our opponents or if it is only symbolic. Unless we were clear about our expectations at the beginning, our membership can be divided when things get tough;
- we have is a specific focus for the action — stopping a road, or timbering or a nuclear generating station, getting housing for the homeless, getting a more efficient public transit system;
- we have enough inside information on our opponents' plans to anticipate their reactions to our action. There is nothing worse than being in an occupation, with no information about how our opponent is responding; or
- we can arrange significant media attention (and therefore public aware- ness) for our action.

The following are a few suggestions for effective blockades and occupa- tions:

- In Canada, many blockades and occupations take place in wilderness areas or remote industrial parks. We need to make sure that participants and supporters know exactly how to get there and that there is sufficient shelter, toilets, parking, food and warmth for everyone who comes. The magnitude of arranging for transportation and everyday life can be overwhelming for some groups. We also need a good system for com- municating with the outside world.
- We should gear the extent of the blockade/occupation to a realistic assessment of support. People may be arrested and removed almost as soon as they arrive. Most people have to work at regular jobs, or have kids to look after, or have other struggles they are deeply engaged in; civil disobedience will take them away from this. Quite often the very people who need to engage in this kind of action have immigration is- sues or criminal records or are on probation or parole (often because of the class and race biases of the court system) and will face more severe repercussions than others if arrested.
- We need to humanize the opposition. The Teme-Augama people opened their second blockade with a Remembrance Day service and invited the provincial police officers to join in the service. One of the elders then

spoke about the role of the police, who had to do the "dirty work for the people who make the policies." He made an appeal to them to support the blockade. By the end of the blockade, even some construction workers were sabotaging their own equipment. One organization suggests beginning an occupation in an office building by presenting flowers to the receptionist and apologizing for messing up her day.

- We need to be clear that decisions about continuing the action or what to do during the action can be made by the people on the frontline. Affinity groups work best.
- We need to be prepared to work through the court system after the blockade, because people are bound to be arrested; we have to have good legal advice lined up.
- The power structure learned a long time ago that boredom can become as effective as fear in disorganizing as a group. We can use the time during the action for educational, cultural and social group building and to show the public how things could be done if it weren't for the primacy of the profit motive.

Disciplined non-violent direct action is an assertion of our responsibility to care for one another and the land when governments fail to do so. It is a sacred act.

Note

1. Starhawk, *Webs of Power* (Gabriola Island, BC: New Catalyst Books, 2002) p. 212.

16

Taking on the Bigger Picture

Decades of being told by our media and elites that all politicians are corrupt and self-serving, that the public does not matter, that private enterprise does everything better and that all public servants are self-seeking have trashed most of the respect the public had for government service and politics. This is a tragedy. Government has the power to raise money with taxes, to borrow against the future, to determine our foreign policy (including wars), to prop up and subsidize industry, to fund civil society and to determine the nature of policing. When progressive people do not seriously engage in government, we leave governance to the corporations. We cannot afford to do this.

Governance is a process, not a thing. The institution and functioning of governance is made up of consenting human labour — on the readiness of people to just "do their job," whether they are clerks, assistant deputy ministers, researchers, scientists or members of Parliament. Those people who go against the current, who raise their voices and find ways to pull some justice and integrity from the structure are brave indeed. As organizers, it is our job to build the movements that find the means to strengthen the ability of people to assert their values, to enable them to question the system in which they work, to allow them to support the movements for systemic change.

There can be no doubt that the process of governing has been pretty well captured by the corporations and the elites in Canada. However, it is not an option to abandon it. We need governance of some sort, and in the absence of a functioning alternative to replace it, we need to try to change what we have. Even in the most destitute and corrupt countries in the Global South, people take government seriously: they know it matters.

Decisions about which issues movements take up and how we organize are, in the end, decisions about the kind of future we want to build. When we direct our demands at corporations, asking them to be "responsible," we are making a statement that corporations are capable of having a social conscience. In fact, it has been shown in a number of studies on corporate social responsibility initiatives that they only happen when a company is worried that it will be regulated or when it is worried about maintaining the loyalty of its employees.[1]

When, on the other hand, we direct our demands to our government, we are making a statement that we expect our elected representatives and public servants to be accountable to those of us who elected them and who pay taxes for them to spend, and we are saying that we will do everything in our power to ensure they act in our interests.

Despite declining voter turnouts, people in Canada are not ready to give up on government; they just want it to work better. Even as the corporate juggernaut has strengthened, our ability to influence government has provided some protection for the environment and for the most vulnerable people. There still are some decent politicians, dedicated and honest public servants and worthwhile government programs. Only the most cynical would say that we should abandon these. Who knows how many times organized Canadians have already saved this country from the worst excesses of corporate power?

A rational extension of our work to build communities and a culture of environmental and social justice at the local level is to support movements for the kind of systemic changes that would transform governance at the federal and provincial levels in Canada. Such transformations won't happen unless we take the time to build a broad-based movement to press for these changes. These demands include proportional representation, laws to limit corporate charters and curb the power of corporations, effective environmental protection, ecological full-cost accounting, participatory budgeting, the protection of the commons, equity and justice in social programs and taxation, Aboriginal sovereignty and the redirection of military spending.

Municipal Governments

Municipal government is the logical focus for community-based organizing in Canada. Municipalities can initiate decisions around public transportation systems, city planning, alternatives to the "social safety net," housing, recreation and neighbourhood centres. They can determine the level of democracy at a grassroots level in the neighbourhoods and the city itself. In cities like Porto Alegre in Brazil, the municipal budget is now determined by a mass participatory process;[2] we should be able to organize for that here too.

In cities where there have occasionally been good mayors and strong councils, the difference is palpable. But these victories have always come about as a result of mass organizing and engendering excitement about the possibilities of change in a broad spectrum of people. Because it has to defeat the developer lobby, a principled win in municipal elections depends on the work of many active citizens.

Like any other institution, the bureaucracy that actually runs municipal government and school boards is subject to pressures from the corporate sector (mostly land developers) and the public. Our job is to increase public knowledge, enthusiasm and pressure, and to understand how the city works and where systems can be changed to make it function in the public interest.

Usually, very few people vote in municipal elections, so the trick is to grab the attention of voters with issues that matter to them and will motivate them to vote. We need to know who our supporters are and get them to the polls. An excellent example of this kind of work is done by Education Action in Toronto.[3]

The Riverdale model (three canvasses of the entire ward) has also been found to be highly effective. It is labour intensive and so is only possible with a lot of real community support. The first canvass is with a short leaflet when the candidates announce they are running. The second, in person with a more sophisticated leaflet, continues throughout the campaign. The third, a reminder to vote, giving details of the polling station, goes to supporters and undecided voters in the last week. Candidates call on as many people personally as possible. Social media has been used effectively in some campaigns. On voting day, those persons who were found to be supportive, are called, reminded to vote and offered help getting to the poll.

The ability to do anything once we get on council is directly proportional to the level of organization in the neighbourhoods. Having sympathetic politicians in office is of very little use unless they are one part of a much larger organization. Getting representatives elected is key to an overall organizing strategy, but they have to be accountable to the movement that gets them into office.

Just the process of being elected changes how the candidates think about themselves. It is easy for a person to let the position go to their head: to think they know more than the people; to get wrapped up in "how complicated the whole system is"; to become a broker between the power structure and the community organization, instead of their representative. Representatives need help from a movement with research and choosing priorities. Good municipal councillors need community support and pressure to help them stand up against the local elites.

Participating in National and International Movements

Transnational corporations, working with their client governments, have been instrumental in the creation of international institutions and agreements like the World Bank, the North American Free Trade Agreement and the World Trade Organization to regulate trade, investment and knowledge to ensure the satisfaction of their voracious appetite for resources, capital and labour. Groups set up by the United Nations like the Food and Agriculture

Organization, the Global Compact and so on become sites of struggle between corporate interests and the rest of us.

When we organize on local issues, we cannot ignore these behemoths. It is a little like ants trying to create a home in an elephant enclosure. Although we might scare them off for awhile, we are still likely to be trampled. The elephants are so big, we don't even know what they look like. We only see the bottom of the foot and the damage it leaves when it comes down.

Fortunately, there are a number of organizations (for example, the Council of Canadians, the Polaris Institute, GRAIN and the ETC Group) that specialize in understanding how these institutions and agreements work and in translating what they are doing into language we can understand. They have staff and members who travel to the big international meetings and gather intelligence for us. They put us in touch with other communities all over the world that are fighting battles similar to ours. They play a crucial role in shifting power.

Some of these organizations help organize the huge anti-globalization protests and gatherings around the world, like the World Social Forums and Climate Justice Action. A network of international activists and organizations create the spaces for these events to happen. For community activists to go to these gatherings can be a fantastic experience: we are surrounded by and able to learn from thousands of people who are working on many different parts of the alternative society. Understanding we are part of a global movement for change is essential to building our strength. However, the power of a movement lies in the capacity of the communities and groups that compose it. Although work on the national and international level is important, it will go nowhere unless we build the base at home. It is a question of where we put our energy: some people will want to do the networking and travel, but a lot more of us need to do the hard slogging where we live.

All of the larger NGOs have their own issue-based agenda, and they are usually hungry for case studies and examples to support it. Most of us will probably agree with their agenda and we probably think that getting attention on our community issues will help us achieve our goals. However, using our community as a case study for a big NGO can create problems at home, and these should be thought about and discussed before we get involved. Getting increased national and international attention to our community issue may escalate matters beyond what we can absorb in our strategy: there may be a flurry of media attention and a sophisticated government or corporate response that we cannot decode.

Once the other organization takes up our issue, we may lose control of it. We may find that the organization is expecting us to host a number of visitors or to travel to speak (with them) about the issue. They may not represent our concerns accurately or may only be interested in the part that fits with their agenda and nothing else. They may be using their links with us to raise money for their organization in a way that prevents us from raising money for our community itself. Most seriously, the larger organization might negotiate on our behalf without our consent. Or, after we have come to depend on their interest, they might change their strategy and drop us. This can be devastating for our members.

So, we need to be aware of the networks and movement activists that work on the global issues that touch our community. We need to learn from them, find ways to explain why these issues matter at home and participate in exchanges, gatherings and demonstrations where we can afford the time and money to do it. If we participate through a larger issue-based organization, we need to ensure that our community is in control of the agenda and that this is a partnership, not a client relationship. We need to be careful about dependency.

Systems of Oppression at Home

When I was retiring from MiningWatch Canada in 2008, we advertised for someone to take over the Canada Program of the organization. The ad clearly specified that we wanted someone with experience working in Canada. Out of 135 applicants, we only got three who had actually worked for social and ecological justice in Canada or who even expressed an interest in working here. Almost all of the applicants were young people who were passionately interested in international development; many of them had done work in the Global South. Most did not even show an interest in understanding the issues here, although a few mentioned an interest in "helping" Aboriginal communities.

However, if we work with communities in the Global South, almost all their leaders will beg us to work in Canada, to change the behaviour of the "developed" countries that are disorganizing them and pillaging their resources. They don't think that Canadians have much to offer them in terms of advice or community practice. In their view, it is the power structures in Europe and North America that need to change. So why is there a lack of interest in working in Canada? Do we find our own country boring? Do we think it will be impossible to do anything? Do we not recognize our own complicity? Or do we just not know where to start?

Working to change law and regulation in Canada is the way we can most effectively support those working for change in other countries: our issues are intrinsically linked, and changing the way power operates here will provide space that the people of Africa, Latin America and Asia need to reclaim their economies, their cultures and their very lives for themselves. The problem is not the "poor," it is "impoverishment," the accumulation of wealth and power in the hands of a global elite — some of whom live here in Canada. When it comes to resource extraction — oil and gas, mining, corporate agriculture — Canada is an international predator.

We must never forget that community activists in the Global South who are struggling for their children's future rely for their survival on the work of their supporters in the North, on the turbulence and dissent that we can create in our own countries. Understanding how the structures and institutions which shape our lives work is crucially important if we want to change systems of oppression here at home.

During the birth of MiningWatch Canada we held two conferences. The first, only five months after we opened, was a consultation with Indigenous leaders, sponsored by the Innu Nation, a founding member of MiningWatch, to share what they had learned so far from the experience with Voisey's Bay. The conference, called Caught Between a Rock and a Hard Place, helped us understand the issues facing Indigenous communities in Canada. Many of the people who attended (including the Innu) were willing to have mining on their lands, and some already did. Others were adamantly opposed.

The second conference, less than a year later, was a consultation with representatives of Indigenous communities around the world affected by mining. In both cases, we asked the participants what they thought the new MiningWatch should be doing. Since at least 60 percent of mining was taking place on lands that were still under Indigenous control, we felt we needed their direction and permission before we could really go forward.

The findings of the two conferences were remarkably similar. The communities insisted on being in control of any solidarity work. They wanted us to provide research on mining companies and how the industry worked. They wanted us to help get the story of their struggle out to the world in a way that built support for their cause. They wanted us to change Canadian laws to get companies under control and to protect the lands, waters and people where their mines were.

What we learned from them was that leadership for a vision of real change would come from the Global South, from the Indigenous people who still remembered the Original Teachings, who were taking responsibility for the protection of their traditional lands and who were resisting the predations of Canadian mining companies with creativity and courage.

Solidarity with the Global South (and Indigenous people in Canada) means working to change those systems which disorganize and pillage communities. It means understanding the structural causes of their situation. Those structures are headquartered where those of us in the North live. They are maintained by our cultural constructs and our economic and political system. It is we who benefit from the misery of the rest of the world. When we know this, we can see that it is our responsibility to dismantle those structures of oppression where we live — to organize for justice, peace and the integrity of creation in the communities in the country that we call home.

Notes

1. Moira Hutchinson, *Canadian NGO Policy Views on Corporate Responsibility and Corporate Accountability* (Ottawa: CCIC, March 2001).
2. Rebecca Neara, "Introduction: Participation, Empowerment, and State-Society Relations," in R. Neara, *Inventing Local Democracy: Grassroots Politics in Brazil Colorado* (Boulder, CO: Lynne Rienner Publishers, 2000) p. 1–22.
3. <www.educationactiontoronto.com>.

Part 6

Lessons Learned

Northern Dreams Quilt

17

Fighting for Hope

Gardening in Sudbury

Driven by dreams of healthy food and beauty,
I began this garden.
Only dead lawn, a few bits of hardy crabgrass and dandelions.
No life in this soil, except the cutworms,
Long destroyed by Gro-green and Killex.
Day after day, pushing my pitchfork into the thatch,
Pulling out the old grass and weeds,
Adding peat moss and manure,
Imported from the countryside —
If there's no life in your soil,
Bring in some outside agitators.
Adding wood ashes from my own fireplace,
Where the winter fires had brought us warmth,
Adding the compost that let us feel
Self-righteous about leftovers.
Then letting it rest for the winter.
While we dreamed through catalogues:
In this inhospitable northern climate, what will grow?
How about Siberian grapes? Nix the luscious kiwi.
Where do we place them, so they don't crowd out the others?
Warding off insects, attracting bees, exchanging secrets?
Carrots and tomatoes, sage with cabbage, beans with corn
So they get enough sun, enough shade,
So we can get at them for the harvest?
In the spring, waiting for the frost to end,
We turn the soil again, add more nutrients, make the beds.
Holding fast to the vision of
Soil, sun, rain, seeds, insects and
Gardener, producing together.

The planting itself doesn't take very long.
For a few weeks, we watch the garden
Will it to grow.
Some seeds don't come up.
Some are lopped off by cutworms.
I turn predator, dig into the soil,
Crush them between my finger and thumb.
Where soil is saturated with past chemicals
The plants are stunted and sick.
Brown-spotted broccoli, shrivelled squash,
Maggots destroy an entire crop of onions.
Acid from the belching super-stack
Deep-sixes the irises.
The war with the earwigs over the corn crop
Finds me in the store flirting
With Roach motels and Raid cans.

But other plants thrive.
Beans inundate us with green plenty.
The kids say "catsup" means
"Catch up with the tomatoes,"
Lettuce and endive and potatoes and beets
And carrots and corn and cukes.
Jaunty marigolds and daisies.
Herbs for healing and protection.
Vagabond pumpkins in the compost.
Wood sorrel and lamb's quarters between the rows.
And this is just our first year of work.
With the same care, it will be better next year…
More poisons gone, more life-giving soil,
A more knowledgeable gardener.
More ability to sustain ourselves,
More resistance to disease and death,
And, soon, the time is coming I promise you,
We will grow our own seeds.

Conclusions

At this time, we are faced with the need to create a society that can live in harmony with the earth, that sees human beings as one part of creation. We have to recognize, understand and transform the systems that have fostered destruction and exploitation.

It is in our long-term self-interest to live respectfully with the earth and one another, and most people try to do this. But we have lost our way. We have taken many roads that look seductive but lead to injustice, ecological destruction and misery. The challenge for those of us living in the belly of the beast is to enable the people who share our space to be the agents of their own future.

All people want to be able to deal with what life visits on them and their loved ones, and all people want to create the changes they need and to resist those that hurt them. Most of us want power, not the power to dominate and control others but power-with, the ability to work and act together. Politics is the organization of power. There is a politics of the family, of the church, of the classroom and of the community just as there is a politics of the state or the global economy. The systems of domination are enshrined in our daily lives.

In our desperation about the current global ecological and financial crises, it is easy to take up counter-productive strategies that increase fear in the general public, dismiss the important community-building and small project work as "reformist" and make appreciating the concept of the "public good" or "the commons" more difficult. Our meetings are often fraught with anger, dogma and factionalism. We need to step back and begin to work holistically.

The economic, social and political systems we live in have been created and are maintained by human labour, and they depend on our consent. The work of organizers is to create an environment where people feel they have to withhold their consent, where they can refuse to cooperate with oppression, where they have the relationships and skills to resist collectively.

Leadership to transform corporate power is still vested in small numbers of people, but we need the support of the majority to make the changes we need to save human life on the planet. The social change project in Canada is failing where it does not engage new people in the movement or build support for our causes and analysis with the general public. Many small victories are the stuff of which change is truly made. People are lonely and afraid; they are propagandized and diverted by advertising culture; their work is unfulfilling. Our task is to reach out to others in order to build relationships of dignity and respect, to create new means to care for one another and to create environments where people are able to talk about and act to save human life on this planet, including being able to withhold their consent from the corporate juggernaut.

People do not get involved in the change project for many good reasons: fear in all its forms, the worship of wealth and greed, media propaganda that diverts us from the important questions in life and makes us despair about making change, workplaces that teach us we are stupid and the lack of any real experience of community in our daily lives. When we do begin to have some success, we have to deal with sophisticated techniques for co-opting and misleading our organizations.

Place-based organizing works. If we start the re-building of community in those places where we choose to put our allegiance, then we are able to make links between the physical world around us and the people, animals and plants living in it. We will find it harder to ignore our neighbours or to avoid those with whom we are uncomfortable. The Other is less frightening. In place-based organizing, we can assist one another in material ways — shelter, water and food, warmth, transportation, childcare and elder care, home repair, advocacy. This tangible work to care for one another can lead to new relationships and new institutions and creates safe places to learn different ways of looking at the world.

Organizers have to like and respect the people they work with. Our job is to find ways to build the agency of ordinary folk to work together to change our political and economic institutions for the better, for the healing and protection of the earth and for justice. As people have experiences where they are treated with dignity and respect, the capacity to recognize root causes and to act together for change grows. The challenge for organizers is to enable and create these experiences.

We start by listening for the causes and ideas that are important to our neighbours and then bring people who share similar concerns together to act. There is no substitute for the hard work of neighbourhood organizing. Going door-to-door with a questionnaire is only one way to do this. More effective is using the "snowball" technique: asking someone who has talked with you, who else in the neighbourhood they would suggest you talk to. People may want to build a park; they may be bored teenagers; they may want to stop a mine or get rid of dump; they may want to find elder care or build a community garden. Organize potlucks, build friendships at a local level, help one another with crises as they arise.

Our communities will choose the causes they want to work on. If we build on what the community unites to do, the work will stimulate enthusiasm and a desire to continue. It's how we organize that counts. We need to organize in a way that listens and builds capacity to act. We find creative ways to help the community see how local issues are related to broader issues of power and control, and to find allies and strategies to take them on.

We develop groups that encourage a feeling of "we." We build social energy from within and do not depend on an "enemy" for their cohesion. We make sure the group size and form is appropriate to the work.

Some organizational forms bring out the good in us, and some bring out the bad. More attempts at change and community building fail because we cannot get along with each other than for any other reason. We have all internalized the competitive, racist, sexist and hierarchical parts of our society, and they get in our way even when we work for change. Our meetings, gatherings and events have to reflect our values. We deal with issues of cliques, scapegoats and trouble-makers in a principled fashion.

If we broaden the movement we can reclaim our political, environmental, social and cultural life. We can build a movement of committed people based in orga-nized communities to push for what we need. There are growing numbers of models and tools from all over the world that show us how. We can use an economics that has no "externalities," that does not depend on growth but on healing the damage already caused to the life systems we depend on. We can develop locally owned and controlled food, shelter and energy systems. We can create non-hierarchical workplaces. We can assert and shape political power and enable regulatory change to happen. We can begin to get control of those institutions of power that are open to us in government.

We need to change the systems of oppression here at home. We are much more likely to be able to affect our home environment, if we take the time to research and unpack it, than to affect a foreign one. In Canada, since the systems and structures in our country create misery and oppression in others, we are morally obligated to work to change these systems at home.

Community organizing is a way of life and a trade, with a set of values and tools that are learned through apprenticeship, reading and the experience of doing. The systems of power-over are resisted in our daily lives. We find ways to free ourselves from work that destroys so that we have the time and resources to organize.

We seek ways to support one another financially, but if we do find funding to begin this kind of work, it has to be on our own agenda. Central to building a movement is developing the willingness of participants to put their own money, time and energy into it.

We learn from and work with a common vision of how we want the world to be:

- Our groups work holistically. We pay attention to the cultural, spiritual, economic and environmental health of the ourselves, our families, our communities and the planet. We reconnect with the ancient teachings of the earth.
- We tell the truth about what we need and what is in the way, and — knowing that knowledge is power — we research how to get there.
- We develop a vision worth living our lives for, created out of the struggles for environmental justice of people around the planet, and we broadcast our dreams.
- We create an environment with our work where people can feel at home with a new way of thinking, and where people are ready to risk and learn from one another. We make our meetings places where democracy hap-pens and that create social energy and enthusiasm. We laugh and play with one another.

- We build empowering organizations to sustain the work in communities. We create our own media forums.
- We develop programs and activities together which build community security in economic and political terms: caring for one another, food, housing, health, energy, transportation and dealing with our wastes.
- We develop effective and creative strategies and tactics that reflect what we want the world to look like and that recognize the dance between the forces for liberation and hope and the systems of domination and control.
- We stay linked into networks and broad movements for social change regionally, nationally and internationally. We are aware of the networks and movement activists that work on the global issues that touch our communities. We learn from them, find ways to explain why these issues matter at home, participate in gatherings and demonstrations where we can afford the time and money to do it.
- We work in solidarity with the Global South — in Canada and internationally — to change those systems which disorganize and pillage their communities as well as ours, and to end our complicity in their suffering.

Anishinaabe elder Art Solomon wrote in 1990:

> Yes, we must engage in the dance of life.
> We must liberate ourselves from stifling institutions
> And begin to celebrate our humanity together.
> Because life was not given for us to endure
> But to celebrate.
> And God's dream for us will not be accomplished
> By hiding in our dark corners
> And shaking in our boots.
> Listen to the teachers, the young ones,
> They're saying we want a new world,
> But we need it right now.
> Do we need to wait and talk about it first?
> Or just get up and do it?
> Time will not wait for us
> And those involved in the game of death
> Could get us hooked
> Because it's the "only game around."
>
> I have an abiding faith in the God
> That I pray to;
> That [God] is not going to allow Creation
> To be destroyed by the hands of fools.[1]

Note

1. Arthur Solomon, "A Vision for Now," *Songs for the People: Teachings on the Natural Way* (Toronto: NC Press Ltd., 1990) p. 116.

Resources

Resources for Community Organizing are available online at the following website: http://fernwoodpublishing.ca/community/